INCITEMENT TO DISAFFECTION

A Cobden Trust Study

by Thom Young
assisted by Martin Kettle

Acknowledgements

This study is a revised version of a dissertation submitted by Thom Young in October 1975 to the School of Peace Studies, University of Bradford. The manuscript was revised for publication by Martin Kettle, who also wrote much of the last chapter.

The author would like to thank Professor Adam Curle and Dr Uri Davis of the School of Peace Studies for their help during the research; Nigel Siederer, William Birtles and James Klugmann for reading all or part of the manuscript, and offering many useful suggestions; the NCCL for permission to study their archives; the Controller of H.M. Stationary Office; the staffs of the Public Record Office, the British Museum Newspaper Library, the National Library of Scotland, and Mr Norman Higson, Archivist of the University of Hull Library, for their general assistance; various friends in Hull, London and Edinburgh for accommodation; and Margaret Young, for typing the original manuscript.

The Cobden Trust would like to thank the Joseph Rowntree Social Service Trust for its generous assistance in the preparation of this study.

THOM YOUNG is a law graduate from Edinburgh University. He has recently completed an MA at Bradford University.
MARTIN KETTLE is the Research Officer of the Cobden Trust.

Cobden Trust, 186 King's Cross Road, London WC1X 9DE

Printed by The Russell Press Limited (TU), 45 Gamble Street, Nottingham NG7 4ET. Tel: 0602 74505

ISBN 0 900137 08 8

'Whatever rights of free speech and persuasion may be allowed by the governing classes in matters affecting propaganda amongst the civilian population, there is always the widest possible restraint on any kind of propaganda – at least of a distributing character – amongst the armed forces. In the history books supplied to the boys in the Army and in the newspapers there may be flagrantly untrue accounts of the history of the Empire, of the wars in which this country has been engaged, and of other matters in which it might be thought that the truth is important, but let anyone suggest to a member of the forces that this duty to humanity might lead him to disobey orders, and the propagandist will soon find out what is meant by freedom of expression.'

W.H. Thompson: *Civil Liberties* p21

Contents

Introduction

In 1795 Mr Wyndham, Secretary for War, faced a motion of censure in the Commons for having spent millions of pounds of public money in setting up permanent barracks for troops without the permission of the House. In justification he stated that 'he was desirous that the soldiers should be considered as citizens; and in order that they might be so considered, he would withdraw them from bad lessons and dangerous counsel: he would in that case, act by them as he would his own family, his own children.' According to the same gentleman, the simple rationale for the isolation was 'if I cannot make him dumb, I will make you deaf.'[1]

From that time the paternalism of the state has remained almost absolute in relation to the armed forces. Members of those forces are still in law regarded as citizens, but the control which the state exercises over them renders this principle purely nominal. There are two ways in which the state exercises this control: through the authoritarian structure and organisation of the armed forces and by restricting the communications between civilians and members of the Forces.

This study is an attempt to trace the development of the statutory provisions of the criminal law which set out these restrictions on the activities of civilians in relation to employees of the State. It does not specifically deal with the internal control of the armed forces. These statutory provisions supplement the Common Law of Sedition, an extremely vague and dangerous offence which almost defies definition; they are extensions of, but not part of, the Law of Sedition.

Largely because of its relative obscurity, few books on Criminal Law have dealt with this area in any depth and it has been necessary, therefore, to turn to a variety of sources for the material which makes up this investigation. Few of the cases discussed have appeared in the law reports and wherever possible I have made use of newspaper reports to supplement information derived from other publications. In the part relating to the period from the First World War until 1934 I have also been able to include a considerable amount of material from the Public Record Office which was not available in any published form and, as far as I am aware, has not been included in any other work. Thorough search of the relevant indexes revealed no material relating to the subject in any of the records of the Home Office, Air Ministry, or Admiralty. References are to Cabinet papers, conclusions and Committees and to War Office files.

I have also searched the archives of the National Council for Civil Liberties and have included reference to that source in the section dealing with the Incitement to Disaffection Bill, 1934.

Thom Young

Incitement to Mutiny Act 1797

On 1 June 1797 a message from George III was presented to the Houses of Parliament requesting them 'to make more effectual provisions for the prevention and the punishment of all traitorous attempts to excite sedition and mutiny in His Majesty's naval service, or to withdraw any part of His Majesty's forces by land and sea from their duty and allegiance to him, and from that obedience and discipline which are so important to the prosperity and safety of the British Empire.'[2]

It was already an offence at common law to persuade or entice soldiers or sailors to desert from His Majesty's service. According to William Pitt, speaking in the House of Commons in 1797, this offence was originally a common misdemeanour but had been revised and altered so that it carried an additional penalty,[3] making the offender liable in 1797 to imprisonment for six years, during which time he could be set in the pillory twice.[4] Although the royal demand was for 'more effectual provisions', Pitt was clearly of the opinion that English common law did not proscribe the persuasion of soldiers or sailors to other actions contrary to the interests of His Majesty, such as mutiny. This was presumably also the view of the legal authorities of the day. Certainly Stephen in his *History of the Criminal Law of England,* published in 1883, declared that it is remarkable that the offence of endeavouring to seduce soldiers from their duty and allegience to His Majesty, which 'obviously requires the severest punishment . . . was so long unknown to the law.'[5] The Common Law of Scotland also appears to be limited to persuasion to desert.[6]

The circumstances which gave rise to the royal demand for legislation were that two mutinies had broken out in the Fleet at Spithead and at the Nore, but that the crews at the Nore, 'notwithstanding the repeated offers of His Majesty's gracious pardon', had refused to accept the benefits which had enticed those at Spithead to return to service. These events struck fear deep into the hearts of the English oligarchy. In the midst of a financial crisis which involved suspension of gold payments, they had been deserted earlier in the year by all their continental allies and now faced the imminent threat of French invasion. Had it not been for the difficulties of Channel crossings, aggravated to some extent by French Naval and Military incompetence, the various landings in Wales and Ireland would have been far more powerful and possibly more successful. The power, the very existence of the English oligarchy, depended on the English Navy, and specifically on the loyalty of that navy. Suddenly, after years of confidence and complacency on the part of the Executive and poverty and misery on the part of the sailors, that loyalty was questioned.

For a long time the Executive had been attempting to stamp out the activities of the corresponding societies and reform societies but without notable success. Only three years before they had seized the leaders of the principal reform societies for High Treason. Thomas Hardy, Samuel Adams, Jeremiah Joyce, John Thelwall, Daniel Adams and John Horne Tooke had all been tried, and later freed amid jubilation. Increasing social unrest, now taking the form of massive demonstrations and riots in the streets of London, did not help the English ruling class feel at ease. The immediate threat was not merely the possibility of armed invasion from revolutionary France, it was that the obnoxious democratic ideas of revolutionary France might penetrate from across the Channel. Pamphlets and hand-bills preaching democratic doctrines were abundant at this time and the mere suspicion that there might be propagandists at work amongst the Navy was sufficient to merit immediate action. As Hobhouse put it in the Commons, 'That the discontents of the seamen should break out precisely at the same point of time is a strong presumption that their origin is to be attributed to the same malignant authors. Another fair ground of presumption may be derived from the known character of the seamen, a frank and generous race, incapable of forming any deliberate plan of treachery.'[7]

Hobhouse's platitudes were predictable. The Executive, and the Admiralty in particular, were very keen to explain unrest in terms which absolved them from responsibility. Alien agitators furtively distributing seditious propaganda were just the scapegoats they needed to draw the public gaze away from the revelation of a shocking state of administrative incompetence. The sailors were protesting against their own abject poverty and against deplorable conditions on board the ships. Loyalty in such circumstances would have been pathetic. Some crew members undoubtedly were looking over their shoulders towards France, but had their sole motivation been political it is unlikely that they would have been content to bide their time until the Admiralty came to negotiate.

The Government was unable to invoke direct and immediate repression in the form of prosecutions, convictions and exemplary punishments for two reasons: first, because they had not found any specific individual to make the object of such repression, and second, because they did not appear to have the power. This chink in their armour astounded the ruling class, who immediately resolved to rectify the omission. Having survived a vote of censure, the Pitt Government introduced an Incitement to Mutiny Bill to provide severe penalties for this crime, which according to the Prime Minister, 'exceeded the bounds of ordinary treason'.[8] In fact, it was not the seduction of soldiers which was made the substantive offence but endeavouring to seduce them.

Pitt himself was at great pains to justify the Bill, admitting at one stage that 'if any person required substantial evidence of any individual malpractices to excite sedition and mutiny in His Majesty's service, it was not at present in his power to produce it; but he trusted it would be enough to satisfy the House of the necessity for the Bill if the frequency of seditious practices were notorious'.[9] He originally proposed that the crime should constitute an aggravated species of misdemeanour, leaving to the discretion of the court the power of inflicting not only the penalties of fines and imprisonment as in other cases of misdemeanour, but also as the circumstances required, the additional penalties of banishment and transportation. In fact, the Act as passed created yet another capital felony to add to the 350 or so already existing.

After reciting in its preamble, 'divers wicked and evil disposed persons, by the publication of written or printed papers, and by the malicious and advised speaking, have of late industriously endeavoured to seduce persons serving in His Majesty's forces by sea and land from their duty and allegience to his Majesty, and to incite them to mutiny and disobedience.' Section One of the statute enacted that:

> any person who shall *maliciously and advisedly* (my italics) endeavour to seduce any person or persons serving in his Majesty's forces by sea or land from his or their duty and allegience to his Majesty, or to incite or stir up any such person or persons to commit any act of mutiny, or to make or endeavour to make any mutinous assembly, or to commit any traiterous or mutinous practice whatsoever, shall, on being legally convicted of such an offence be adjudged guilty of felony . . . [10]

The *Incitement to Mutiny Act 1797,* therefore, creates not one but four district offences:

First: endeavouring to seduce a person or persons serving in His Majesty's forces by land and sea from his duty and allegience to His Majesty.

Second: endeavouring to incite such a person or persons to an act of mutiny.

Third: endeavouring to incite such a person or persons to make, or endeavour to make any mutinous assembly.

Fourth: endeavouring to incite such a person or persons to commit any traitorous or mutinous practices.

It may seem surprising in view of the subsequent history of this offence that Pitt should have proposed two limiting amendments to his original Bill. The first introduced the requirement that the offence should be committed 'maliciously and advisedly', thus requiring the prosecution to prove that the offence was committed intentionally and that the accused knew that the object of his or her endeavours was a person serving in the forces of the Crown. The second amendment limited the duration of the Act to one month after the commencement of the next session of Parliament.

It was clearly the hope of the Government that the existence of a severe penalty would act as a deterrent and that the infliction of that punishment would be exemplary. That the first prosecution under the Act should take place only a month after its passage hardly justified their faith in its deterrent effect, but it did vindicate their claims and consequently their fears. In this case (*R. v Fuller* [1797], 2 Leach 790), the accused had given a soldier in the Coldstream Guards 'several inflammatory and seditious handbills, entitled "Soldiery", and calculated to incite the army to mutiny, saying at the same time, that they were true copies of every man's heart that wished the country well'. This soldier, apparently feeling 'all the indignation of a true and honest soldier at this base attempt to render him treacherous to his King and Country' took Fuller to his sergeant whereupon Fuller simply attempted to incite the sergeant too. He was convicted and hanged.

The only other reported case relating to the Act before the twentieth century is *R. v Tierney* ([1804], Russell and Ryan 74). The only facts which appear from the report are that Tierney was charged with endeavouring to seduce one James Brown from his duty and allegience to His Majesty. Brown was a sailor who had been in hospital for more than thirty days and was no longer entitled to pay nor liable for what he then did to a court martial. After some doubt, Brown was held to be a person serving in His Majesty's forces within the statute. Tierney was convicted and presumably hanged.

Avowedly a temporary measure, the Act of 1797 was renewed for short periods and eventually lapsed on 1 August 1807.[11] Amid the hysteria of the post-war period, however, a Government Secret Committee investigated the loss of this repressive measure and in 1817 a Bill to perpetuate the Act of 1797 was rushed through Parliament. Such was the panic that it was not until the Bill reached the Lords that a gross drafting error was observed: all the enactments in the expired Act were to be revived and made permanent, although one of them was for limiting the duration of the Act.[12] The Lord Chancellor in 1817 had been responsible for prosecuting Fuller in 1797 and was convinced that the Act had operated as an intimidation ever since. He does not appear to have realised that the Act had expired ten years before.

The permanent enactment of this measure severely restricted freedom of speech and communication by further insulating the armed forces from the political discussions of their fellow countrymen. This was, of course, the legislature's intention. The post-war period was characterised by a new wave of reactionary legislation and practices under the Liverpool administration. It was the era of Peterloo and the notorious 'Six Acts'; it was the hey-day of the political agent provocateur. It is surprising, therefore, that this measure was considered sufficient. So intimidating was it, however, that it was destined to a life of obscurity for the next ninety five years until it was resurrected to serve in the state arsenal of anti-trade union legislation. By then it had been given the short title of The Incitement to Mutiny Act, and the offences were punishable by imprisonment for life or for any shorter period or a fine or both.

The Syndicalist Trials of 1912

The relatively high degree of political liberty which was enjoyed during the first decade of the twentieth century in this country was the result of the continuous struggle which radicals and reformists had waged against their rulers for a century and a half. Cole and Postgate declare with justification 'Speech and political thought were freer than they had ever been before or are today.' and 'The Edwardian age . . . seemed to be an age of ever increasing liberty. Political liberty – "civil liberty" in the common sense – had previously been immense; it was hardly at all interfered with during this period. One serious instance occurred but only one."[13]

That 'one serious instance', the Syndicalist Trials of 1912, was the first use of the Incitement to Mutiny Act since 1804. It is treated by Cole and Postgate as a particularly malicious but isolated set of prosecutions. Yet successful political prosecutions are not only valuable to the State in terms of immediate repression of undesirable actions, ideas and persons, they are also legal precedents. Besides being a return to the infamous prosecutions of the Press almost a century before, these prosecutions were probably the first legal proceedings on account of open trade union propaganda. The First World War deserves recognition as the watershed of civil liberty in this country, but these prosecutions were a clear indication that the tide was already turning.

This revival of the *Incitement to Mutiny Act 1797* was closely linked to the increasing industrial unrest which reached a peak on 1 March 1912 when the miners went on strike to further their demand for a national minimum wage. This was the biggest strike Britain had ever seen; according to the Board of Trade over a million workers were involved. The Syndicalist movement was extremely active at this time urging the workers to cease relying upon Parliament, and advocating militant trade unionism and 'Direct Action'. Such a philosophy was obviously far more alarming and constituted a much more immediate danger to the capitalist state than did the socialism of the Labour MPs.

During 1910 and 1911 the army had been used against strikers in several districts and sometime in 1911 an 'Open letter to British Soldiers', urging them not to shoot strikers if ordered to do so, was published in the *Irish Worker* (see Appendix). This letter was reprinted without comment in the first edition (January 1912) of *The Syndicalist*, the new organ of that movement, from which a railwayman named Fred Crowsley had it reprinted as a leaflet at his own expense. He then personally distributed copies to soldiers at Aldershot, Hyde Park Corner and Hounslow barracks. He was arrested on 31 February and charged under the Act of 1797.[14] Having declared that if he had succeeded in persuading one soldier from being a murderer his labour would not have been in vain, he was committed for trial.

Not content with this prosecution, the authorities indulged in a piece of persecution of a kind unknown in Britain since the early nineteenth century. Guy Bowman, editor of *The Syndicalist*, and B.E. and C.E. Buck, the printers of the paper, had three charges brought against them: two felonies under the Act of 1797, and the common law misdemeanour of 'endeavouring to incite and stir up persons serving in His Majesty's land forces to commit acts of disobedience to the lawful orders of their superior officers.'[15] If this charge was good at Common Law, which is at least open to doubt (although it does not seem to have been questioned in this case) it would indeed be remarkable if the Common Law did not extend to inciting to mutiny. Endeavours to incite to disobedience are clearly not actionable under the Incitement to Mutiny Act. The first offence under Section One of that Act requires, that the endeavour should be to seduce from 'duty *and* allegiance'. Disobedience to lawful orders does not necessarily involve any question of allegiance to His Majesty. Consequently, the common law misdemeanour charged only requires proof of endeavour to seduce from duty and the inclusion of this charge can be seen simply as an attempt to allow for all contingencies. Such slender authority as existed in this area of law was of little assistance to the prosecution in these innovatory proceedings.

Meanwhile, the miners' strike was providing unwelcome instruction in working-class solidarity. Tom Mann, a seasoned militant and leader of the Syndicalist Movement, drew the attention of public meetings in Manchester to the fact that the authorities were having premises prepared as temporary barracks and were concentrating military forces a few miles out of the city. Several times he read out the 'Don't Shoot' letter and declared that he believed in every sentence. At one meeting on 13 March he explained what had happened to Bowman and the Bucks and stated that as he was chairman of the Industrial Syndicalist League, which was responsible for *The Syndicalist*, he did not see how he could escape prosecution.

On returning to London Mann faced the same common law charge as the others and two charges under the 1797 Act were subsequently added.[16] The Attorney-General, Sir Rufus Isaacs, was immediately bombarded with questions in the House and in reply stated that he was desirous of 'prosecuting the person mainly responsible' and that he had consequently authorised the prosecution of Tom Mann. Refusing to withdraw the charges against Bowman and the Bucks, he maintained, 'They are made responsible because they are publishers and printers of (the paper) and that is a matter of defence equally open to them.' In defending these three, Sir Frederick Law, KC, submitted, *inter alia*, that the words of the letter had to be considered 'in the light of the great latitude adopted nowadays'; that an open letter was merely a common form; and that no evidence had been led that a particular number of *The Syndicalist* had ever been communicated to any soldier or anyone serving in the forces of the Crown. Mr. Justice Horridge simply pointed out that the charges were not of success in seducing soldiers, but of endeavouring to do so and all three were convicted, Bowman being sentenced to 9 months imprisonment with hard labour and the Bucks to 6 months with hard labour. These sentences were subsequently reduced to 6 months and one month respectively without hard labour.[17]

On 25 March, Josiah Wedgwood, MP, protested in the House against the institution by the Government of prosecutions of the Press. His speech was a scathing attack on those who were intent on returning to the political prosecutions of a century before. He noted that from 1832 to 1912 – Cobbett to Bowman – prosecutions of the Press of this nature had ceased and that it was from the trial of Cobbett that the freedom of the press really dated. 'The best men in every age have been against such prosecutions', he observed, adding the warning, 'there has always been some provocation, some fear inspiring prosecution. The clamour of propertied classes has again and again deafened the Government to the still, quiet voice of reason and liberty.'[18]

All of this had no effect on the outcome of Mann's trial on 9 May at the Manchester Assizes. Defending himself, Mann stated emphatically that he was compelled to come to the conclusion that these proceedings had been instituted because of his connection with the syndicalist movement; others had written and spoken as he had, but they were not identified with that particular movement and they had not been prosecuted. The Attorney-General had stated in the House that Tom Mann was not being prosecuted for his speeches but because he was ultimately responsible for *The Syndicalist*, in which the letter appeared. His admission of nominal responsibility was used in evidence against him, although what he had said was in reality more an accurate prediction than an admission of actual involvement in publication of the letter. He had not known of the letter's appearance in *The Syndicalist* until after it was on sale; nor was it suggested by counsel for the prosecution that he ought to have been aware of it. His own condemnation of the tactics of the prosecuting authorities had been made to count against him. He was duly convicted and Mr Justice Bankes specifically stated that he was passing the same sentence that Bowman was already undergoing – six months imprisonment (without hard labour).[19]

Although Fred Crowsley's committal proceedings had taken place on 7 March, which was several days before the arrest of the printers and the editor of *The Syndicalist*, and two weeks before Mann's arrest, he was not tried until over a month after Mann. It is certain that the decision to prosecute the others was taken as a result of the evidence in Crowsley's case. This in itself is hardly objectionable, but the conduct of the proceedings against Crowsley stands in stark contrast to the other trials and lends support to Mann's contention that further proceedings were not instituted simply because of an inherent illegality in the publication of the 'Don't Shoot' letter.

Crowsley was tried on 18 June at the Hampshire Assizes and on being convicted was sentenced to four months imprisonment with hard labour, subsequently reduced to two months without hard labour. After the jury had found him guilty the prosecution intimated that if he was willing to give an undertaking not to repeat the offence, the Crown would not press the charge. Crowsley had no hesitation in stating that his conscience would not permit him to give such an undertaking but Mr Justice Channell indicated before passing sentence that had he done so 'the law might have been vindicated and the offence might have been passed over without punishment'.[20] The learned Judge obviously appreciated that nothing would be gained by punishing this man, even though he had personally distributed two thousand copies of the letter with the avowed intention of inciting soldiers to act as the letter urged them to. He was not a syndicalist and the law had already been vindicated by the sentences passed on Tom Mann and the others who were.

The prosecution of the printers was a particularly insidious action which must be regarded as an attempt to put *The Syndicalist* out of production by intimidating any other prospective printer. In fact, this did not happen, as widespread protest led to the four men being released long before they had served their sentences. Tom Mann was only in prison for seven weeks.

When counsel for the prosecution in the Bowman case remarked that it was hoped an example to others would be made, Sir Frederick Law, KC, retorted that if an example were necessary it ought to be drawn from a higher class. This was an allusion to contemparaneous circumstances which clearly indicated the political and class nature of the proceedings against the syndicalists. During the period from 1912 to 1914 several members of the Unionist Party made speeches about the proposal to grant home rule to Ireland, speeches which were clearly actionable under existing law. Some also engaged in activities such as gun-running and drilling the Ulster Volunteer Force, which were not only illegal, but were a grave and very real threat to the physical and social well-being of the people of Ireland. Discussion of the issues involved would be outside the scope of this study; the important point in the present context is that no legal action was taken against these individuals.

The Home Rule Bill was eventually defeated in March 1914 after a threat of mutiny in the British army at the Curragh, encouraged and incited by Tory politicians whose status assured immunity from prosecution. It was also sufficient protection for the army officers who announced their refusal to obey orders and their intention of resigning their commissions sooner than take up arms against the Ulster loyalists. This elicited a statement of support from Bonar Law, leader of the Unionist Party and future Prime Minister. In the House he declared 'any officer who refuses is only doing his duty'.[21] In a book published in 1938, D.N. Pritt quotes several of the more blatantly 'seditious' or 'treasonable' speeches of two of the most prominent speakers against Home Rule, Sir Edward Carson, and F.E. Smith. A few of his examples enforce the point.

Speaking in County Antrim on 19 September 1912 Carson said: 'Here is what the covenant says – In the event of such a Bill being forced upon us we further solemnly and mutually pledge ourselves not to recognise its authority. I do not care twopence whether it is treason or not; it is what we are going to do.'

Equally confident that he would not be charged with treason, Smith declared on 20 September 1913 that, 'Home rule will be dead for ever on the day when 100,000 men armed with rifles assemble at Balmoral (Belfast).'

Later, at Armagh, on 4 October 1913, he repeated: 'On the day on which there will be in Ulster 100,000 disciplined men armed with rifles, wherever else Home Rule may be talked about, it will never be talked of in Ulster.'

Like Smith, Carson was a lawyer and was well aware of the illegality of their actions. He knew that the Unlawful Drilling Act of 1819, one of the infamous Six Acts, rendered him liable to seven years penal servitude, but he was just as confident as Sir Oswald Mosley two decades later that the Act would not be invoked. On 16 May 1913, he acknowledged that drilling was illegal.

> I was reading an Act of Parliament forbidding it. The Volunteers are illegal, and the Government know they are illegal, and the Government dare not interfere with them.[4] . . Don't be afraid of illegalities; illegalities are not crimes when they are taken to assert what is the elementary right of every citizen, the protection of his freedom, and if anyone tells me I should be ashamed of myself, I tell him it is the motive I live for, and if I am threatened I am prepared to defend myself . . . [5] We will not allow any body of men, whether they call themselves a Parliament or a Government, to take away what we consider essential for the carrying on of our rights and privileges.[22]

This assertion of the right to break the law in order to maintain the status quo clearly distinguishes Carson's philosophy of direct action from that of the syndicalists, who were far from satisfied with the existing social order. The Incitement to Mutiny Act was still an excellent weapon for limiting freedom of speech and communication: the state could at least ensure that undesirable democratic ideas did not permeate that institution whose authoritarian structure was the ultimate safeguard against civilian disaffection.

Although the Liberal Cabinet did discuss the political expediency of prosecuting Carson, Smith and others it is unlikely that the decision against doing so was difficult to reach. Whereas the syndicalists were sentenced to periods of imprisonment, Carson and Smith were destined to serve the State in a variety of capacities. Fourteen months after the Curragh Mutiny, Carson was appointed Attorney-General in Asquith's Coalition Cabinet. He became First Lord of the Admiralty in Lloyd George's administration from December 1916 to June 1917, when he entered the War Cabinet. In 1921, he was created a Lord of Appeal (by virtue of having been a law officer). Smith continued as Carson's deputy in 1915 when he was appointed Solicitor-General. He held this post until 1919 when he earned rapid promotion, becoming, as Lord Baron Birkenhead the Lord Chancellor, head of the English judiciary. In 1921 he was created a Viscount, and in 1922 an Earl. He was also Secretary for India from 1924 to 1928. The contrast with the Syndicalists speaks for itself.

Wartime Emergency Regulations 1914-8

On the outbreak of war in August 1914, Asquith's Liberal Government had the Defence of the Realm Act (DORA) passed, to provide the powers necessary for the Executive to conduct the War. Regulations under the Act were made by Orders in Council and these could be issued forbidding almost every activity which the Government considered harmful; new crimes could thus be created overnight. As the war dragged on these extremely wide powers were increasingly invoked to counter criticism of the Executive and the war effort.

The Regulation with which this study is most concerned is Regulation 42. As originally promulgated on 28 November 1914 it read:

> If any person attempts to cause mutiny, sedition or disaffection among any of His Majesty's forces or among the civilian population he shall be guilty of an offence against these regulations.[23]

No attempt was made to define the concepts involved. What constituted disaffection, or how one attempts to cause mutiny among the civilian population was left up to the court to decide. The requirement of intention (*mens rea*) was not even conceded and any individual whose words were interpreted as being within the meaning of the Regulation (as construed by the Court) would have no defence open to him; it would be of no consequence that he did not know, for instance, that a particular person was a member of the armed forces. By the end of the war that Regulation was even wider in its terms. As of 22 March 1918, it read:

> If any person attempts or does any act calculated or likely to cause mutiny, sedition, or disaffection among any of His Majesty's Forces, or any of the Forces of His Majesty's Allies, or among the civilian population, or to impede, delay or restrict, the production, repair, or transport of war material, or any other work necessary for the successful prosecution of the war, he shall be guilty of an offence against these regulations.[24]

As of 6 September 1916, a Regulation 42A was added making it an offence for any person to attempt 'to induce a member of any of His Majesty's Forces to act in a manner which *such person knows* (my italics) to be in contravention of the King's Regulations (and any other Instructions or Orders relating to the Army, Navy or Air Force).[2] This placed the onus on the prosecution to prove that the accused knew the contents of the King's Regulations relevant to the charge. This would seem to have provided an almost blanket protection, since few individuals would know the contents of those regulations. This is strangely in contrast to Regulation 42, which provided no protection to the many pacifists who were prosecuted under it during the course of the war.

Police powers were far greater during the war than they had ever been before. Regulation 51A (28 July 1915) provided:

> If a justice of the peace is satisfied by information in writing upon oath laid before him by a competent naval or military authority or any person duly authorise by him, or by an officer of police of a rank not below that of inspector, that any document containing any information, report or statement, the publication whereof would be an offence against these regulations has been or is about to be issued for publication or dispersion from, or that copies thereof are upon, any premises, or that preparations are being made on any such premises for the publication of any such information, report, or statement the justice may issue a warrant authorising a constable to enter, at any time, and if need be by force, and search the premises and to seize any such document, and any written or printed copies thereof, and any type or other plant or appliance which has been or is being used or is intended to be used or is capable of being used in the production of such copies or of the publication in which the information, report or statement has appeared or is about to appear and bring them before a court of summary jurisdiction.[25]

The Defence of the Realm Regulations presented the authorities with both the experience of autocratic powers and with a blueprint for the creation of more permanent legislation after the war. Although the armistice came into force at 11 am on 11 November 1918, the war did not officially end until the Peace Treaties had been signed in August, 1921. This legal fiction of continuance of the State of Emergency for three years after the cessation of hostilities justified the retention of the powers assumed to deal with that emergency. The DORA Regulations were far from dead after 1918, and their continued use in peace-time confirmed the belief that the powers conferred by them were essential for the maintenance of 'law and order' in post war society.

By 1918 the 'Bolshevik' had emerged as the latest British bogey-man, to be despised, rooted out, and legislated against. This new threat to national security was introduced to the people of Britain as a major theme in the election of December 1918 when the Conservatives and Liberals, portrayed the Labour Party as Bolshevik led and inspired.[26] Red infiltration, however, was a much more alarming prospect in other institutions. The increased membership, status, power and apparent militancy of the trade unions immediately after the war was obviously a source of concern to the state, the more so since the formation in 1914 of the Triple Alliance of miners, railwaymen, and transport workers had raised the possibility of strike action bringing the industrial life of the country to a standstill. The sentiments of Mr Hobhouse in 1797 were expressed once again: that the docile British workers, who had always been satisfied with their lot, should become discontented at the same time as Bolshevik agitators were supposed to be at work, was clear evidence that the Bolsheviks had *caused* the discontent. The Bolsheviks, it seemed, had infiltrated the Trade Union Movement as well as the Labour Party.

Events in Russia had reminded the British military authorities that any movement seeking to ferment revolution in Britain would attempt to seduce the armed forces from their loyalty to the State. Events in Britain indicated that the military would increasingly be used in strikes. It seemed imperative, therefore, that the armed forces be isolated from both Bolshevik propaganda which might seduce them from their allegiance and also from Trade Union propaganda which might encourage them to sympathise with the working class. In fact, the authorities were not concerned to distinguish different types of propaganda. As will be seen, literally any document which might encourage a soldier to consider his actions in any perspective other than simple obedience to orders was characterised as 'insidious literature'.

In the midst of increasing industrial unrest during 1919 the Lloyd George Government had good reason to be concerned about the loyalty of the guardians of law and order, both the Police and the Army.

Incitement to Disaffection and the Police

From 1913 the Home Office and the Police Authorities had been hostile to the emergent trade union in the Metropolitan Police Force. A strike in 1872 and another in 1890 had resulted in police grievances being satisfied, but a considerable number of strikers had been dismissed on both occasions. Official recognition of the Police and Prison Officers' Union, as it was later called, was consistently refused on the ground that the police had ample opportunity to make any representation they desired to the Commissioner, through their Superintendent. By August 1918, police pay and general conditions of service had so deteriorated and lagged behind that a strike was inevitable in the absence of prompt Government action. The Government failed to intervene at all and the dismissal of a prominent member of the Union on account of his union activities was the final provocation. An ultimatum was presented that unless the Union's demands, including reinstatement of the dismissed constable and recognition of the Union, were met by midnight, 28 August, the men would strike. Such was the inadequacy of the representative machinery, that despite that ultimatum, New Scotland Yard was taken completely by surprise the following day when more than half of the Metropolitan Police Force, numbering 12,000 men, and virtually all the men in the City of London Police Force had withdrawn from duty.[27]

On 31 August, General Smuts, for the Government, offered to negotiate, but he refused to meet the Union Executive and eventually the Prime Minister, Lloyd George, had to intervene, to arrange a settlement with the Executive. The terms of this Settlement included, on the side of the Government, an increase of pay, a non-contributory scheme of widow's pensions, machinery for the representation of grievances, and the right to join the Police and Prison Officers' Union. The men's representatives undertook not to organise with a view to a strike.

Also on 31 August, General Sir Nevil Macready, Adjutant General of the Army, communicated his fears to the Secretary of State for War, Lord Milner, pointing out that 'the Metropolitans being an organised force directly under the Government, any concession made to them in the direction of union recognition would be more than a stepping-stone towards a similar state of affairs in the army, an opportunity which would not be neglected by those who were already making insidious efforts to undermine the discipline of the troops.[28] That afternoon Macready was informed by the Prime Minister that it was 'of National importance' that he should take the post of Commissioner of the Metropolitan Police. He had already had experience of strikes some eight years before when he commanded troops and about four hundred Metropolitan Police gathered to keep order among Welsh miners. He was not the militaristic obscurantist that some critics have portrayed him to be, but his attitude to the Police trade union was one of hostility. No 'Soviet organisation' could ever be permitted in any disciplined force.[29]

He did believe, however, that some sort of representative machinery was essential in a body of men as large as the Metropolitan Police: a view which may be contrasted with that held by his predecessors and at least one of his successors, who believed that the only form of representation to be considered was through the superior officers.

Macready set up a representative Board, elected by the men. When the executive committee of that Board turned out to be the executive of the Union under a different name, he decided to give the scheme the fullest possible latitude, convinced that it would not be long before the leaders would 'proceed to extremes which would disquiet the bulk of the force and bring the whole agitation to a head'.[30] In preparation for the strike which he regarded as inevitable, and which he was guilty of engineering, he drafted orders notifying the force that any man who failed to turn out for duty when called upon would be summarily dismissed. He also made arrangements with the military authorities to occupy ninety 'pivotal police stations' with small detachments of soldiers, 'in order to give protection and confidence to the men who remain loyal'.[31]

Early in 1919 he wrote to the Home Secretary suggesting that separate Boards be set up for Constables, Sergeants, Inspectors, Superintendents and Chief Constables, as the existing scheme was 'prejudicial to discipline'.[32] On 3 March, at a Home Office conference to discuss steps to be taken in case of labour trouble, he caused alarm by admitting that at that time he could not depend on the force in the event of it being called upon to quell labour riots.[33] The Government appointed a committee under Lord Desborough to conduct a full inquiry into conditions of service of the police throughout Britain. An interim report of this committee recommended an immediate increase in pay and the Government introduced a Bill into the House of Commons on 8 July, ostensibly to give effect to this recommendation. The first two clauses, however, sought to replace Macready's Board with a new Police Federation to which all officers below the rank of Inspector were to belong but which was to have no association with any outside body. For the first time since trade unions were emancipated a Government was seeking to suppress a union by Law.

Clause 3 of the Bill which dealt with inciting disaffection amongst the police was re-enacted as Section 25 (1) of the Police Act 1956, and subsequently as Section 53 (1) of the Police Act 1964, and Section 42 (1) of the Police (Scotland) Act 1967. The wording was only slightly altered in the re-enactment:

> Any person who causes, or attempts to cause, or does any act calculated to cause, disaffection amongst the members of any police force, or induces or attempts to induce, or does any act calculated to induce, any member of a Police force to withhold his services or to commit breaches of discipline shall be guilty of an offence.

On 31 July the Executive of the Police Union called a strike, the declared object being to force the Government to withdraw clauses 1-3. Macready, however, had issued his warning order on 31 May in anticipation of the strike and out of seven forces affected (totalling around 50,000) only 2,300 men went on strike, 1,056 of them from the Metropolitan Force. In Liverpool, 932 out of a total of 2,100 came out and the military had to be called in to quell a riot.[34] Railway workers in London and Liverpool declared themselves ready and eager to strike in support of the police believing the Bill to be the thin end of the wedge against unions in general. Having been warned, the strikers were dismissed. The Bill was passed. The union had been suppressed.

There was considerable opposition to the Bill in the Commons but even the Labour Party was not solidly opposed to it. The Home Secretary eulogised the police, declaring that a more loyal body of men never existed, but that (like the armed forces in 1797 and 1817) they had to be protected since they had become 'discontented, ripe even for revolt and unfortunately, rapidly becoming a fertile ground for the doctrines of men of very wild and extreme views. It must have been evident,' he urged in conclusion, 'that something had to be done and done as quickly as possible'.[35]

This Act imposed on the Police the type of organisation which the Government wanted them to have and one which securely isolated them from the Trade Union movement and insulated them against any external undesirable political influence. Despite the fact that the men themselves were not consulted, the Home Secretary insisted that the Federation was fundamentally 'democratic' and that the Act did not affect the liberty of the individual policeman 'in the slightest degree'. 'His liberty remains absolutely,' he assured the House. 'except in so far as it is limited by Clause 2.' He was equally confident that Clause 3 was in no sense a challenge to trade unionism and would not 'reduce the power of trade unionism in so far as it is properly exercised.'[36] In justification of Clause 3 he confided that there were people in the country 'whose methods are of such a nature that it is essential for them to be able to have a disaffected police force that they can rely upon to fail the country during some crisis'. The Home Secretary did not offer a definition of disaffection, and neither does the Act. Nor is the offence under Section 3 limited to causing disaffection. 'An act calculated to induce a policeman to commit a breach of discipline', is so broad that it could conceivably be interpreted as extending to trifling matters. In line with the DORA Regulations quoted above, this section abrogates the traditional requirement to prove *mens rea* (intention), which is particularly objectionable in view of the vagueness of the offences. The refusal by the Home Secretary to accept an amendment requiring the offence to be committed 'wilfully' suggests that the Government was determined that permanent enactments would have as few defences or loopholes available as the Emergency Regulations which were still in force.

It is important to realise that the provisions of Section 3 of the Act rendered illegal criticisms of Section 1 and 2 of the Act. This was the final guarantee of quiescence on the part of former Union officials, since criticism of the Federation or continued agitation for a Police Union could easily be interpreted as 'calculated to cause disaffection'.

The maximum penalties under Section 3 were imprisonment for a period not exceeding two years on conviction on indictment, and for a period not exceeding three months or a fine not exceeding £50 or both on Summary conviction. No change was made in this respect in the Act of 1956, but the Act of 1964, which did not apply to Scotland, introduced the alternative of a fine on conviction on indictment and increased the penalties on summary conviction to imprisonment for a period not exceeding six months or a fine not exceeding £100 or both. Since 1964, therefore, the penalties for this offence have been greater in England than in Scotland. The Act of 1967 did not affect this anomaly since it repeated the penalties of the earlier legislation.

There have been only two prosecutions on charges of attempting to cause disaffection amongst the Police, both under the original provision of 1919. These will be discussed below.

Incitement to Disaffection and the Armed Forces 1918-24

THE TRIPLE ALLIANCE AND THE EMERGENCY POWERS ACT 1920

With Lloyd George's promise of homes fit for heroes ringing in their ears those British soldiers who had survived the fighting in Europe were desperate to return home. The way in which demobilisation was organised caused considerable resentment and mutinies occurred in camps at Calais and Folkestone, while in London some three thousand men marched from Victoria Station and occupied the Horse Guards Parade.[37] In January 1919, the War Office sent a secret circular to commanding officers of troops stationed in Britain, requesting that information on the troops in the area to be sent weekly to the War Office, in order that an efficient Intelligence Service might be established where the Army Council could 'keep its fingers on the pulse of the troops'.[38] The Commanding Officers were asked to answer the following questions for the information of the Secretary of State, Winston Churchill:

Will troops in various areas respond to orders for assistance to preserve the public peace?

Will they assist in strike breaking?

Will they parade for draft overseas, especially to Russia?

They were also requested to provide information on the following:

Whether there is any growth of trade unionism among them.

The effect outside trade unions have upon them.

Whether any agitation from internal or external sources is affecting them.

Whether any Soldiers' Councils have been formed.

Whether any demobilisation troubles are occurring.

This circular came into the hands of the *Daily Herald*, which published it in full on 13 May. The disclosure aroused intense feeling in the trade union ranks and no doubt caused acute embarrassment in Whitehall. *The Times* of 30 May 1919 reported a speech delivered by Churchill in which he attempted to justify the circular:

> The situation then (January 1919) was extraordinarily difficult. We had a considerable number of mutinies in the Army, one at least of a very serious character, in which grave loss of life was happily averted by the tact and courage of all concerned. We had a number of strikes and a great many threats of strikes. There was a threatened railroad strike, and the actual strike which took place all over the tube railways in London. There was a threatened strike of electricians, which was averted only at the last moment. There were serious riots in Glasgow which required the presence of a large number of troops. There was the threatened strike of the Triple Alliance, which was averted by the good sense of all concerned . . .[39]

In order to avoid the possibility of troops being influenced to politically motivated disobedience in action against strikers and at the same time to crush any external agitation for democratisation of the armed forces by the creation of Soldiers Councils or Trade Unions, the War Office Emergency Legislative Committee decided in February 1919 that it would be desirable to continue permanently certain provisions of the DORA Regulations which 'had been found valuable in pracrice'.[40] These were Regulations 42 and 42A quoted above, and Regulation 27 which made it an offence to spread reports or make statements intended or likely to prejudice recruiting for the Army or to prejudice the training, administration, or discipline of the Army. It was originally intended to make possession of documents, the distribution of which would constitute an offence under these Regulations an offence also, but this was deleted for 'prudential reasons'. Significantly, the reference to mutiny and sedition in Regulation 42, was also omitted as unnecessary on account of the Act of 1797.[41]

The remaining provisions were introduced in the House as an amendment to the Annual Army Bill of 1919. Not for the first time, however, the Government had completely misjudged the feeling of the House and amid fierce attack from all sides the impropriety of the measure was realised. It was reluctantly withdrawn in Committee.[42]

Undaunted by this annoying but instructive set-back, the Army Council launched a political crusade for permanent measures to deal with propagandists which was to continue more or less uninterrupted until 1934. In the meantime the DORA Regulations were still in force and the Government had the powers to act, as in September 1919, when a strike brought almost all the railways in the country to a standstill and troops were called out in large numbers.

One more attempt was made in 1919 to legislate in this area. The *Aliens Restriction (Amendment) Act,* passed in December, perpetuated certain DORA Regulations relating to aliens and enacts by Section 3:

1 if any alien attempts or does any act calculated or likely to cause sedition or disaffection amongst any of His Majesty's Forces or the forces of His Majesty's allies, or amongst the civilian population, he shall be liable, on conviction on indictment to imprisonment for a term not exceeding ten years, or on summary conviction to imprisonment for a term not exceeding three months.

2 if any alien promotes or attempts to promote industrial unrest in any industry in which he has not been *bona fide* engaged for at least two years immediately preceding in the United Kingdom, he shall be liable on summary conviction to imprisonment for a term not exceeding three months.

Section 3 (1) is simply a re-enactment of DORA Regulation 42, with the substitution of 'alien' for 'person' and the omission of 'mutiny', which was incongruous in any case. Neither subsections required intention to be proved, and neither of them provided for fines as alternative penalties to imprisonment. Both subsections rendered illegal actions by aliens, which would not have been illegal if committed by British citizens. The Incitement to Disaffection Act 1934 has changed this to some extent, but its maximum penalty is fixed at two years' imprisonment, and it does not cover the forces of other nations.

Section 3 (2) of the 1919 Act is a blatant restriction on otherwise legitimate trade union activity. A suggestion of strike action, even if hypothetical, or the expression of an opinion, for example that a particular job is not well paid, could easily be interpreted as attempts to promote industrial unrest. The section effectively excludes foreigners from union activity unless they have been engaged in one particular industry in the UK for two years. It is of no consequence that they have lived in the UK for a much longer period. Nor would it only apply to someone actually engaged in the industry; an author of a book advocating militant trade unionism in a particular industry could well face charges under Section 3 (2).

It is ironic that this manifestation of post-war xenophobia should remain on the statute book to this day at a time when Governments are endeavouring by statute to integrate all sections of the community.

The passage of this measure seems to have escaped the attention of the members of the Army Council who, in preparing for the Army Annual Bill of 1920, decided to press once more for an amendment on the lines of the previous attempt.[43] Surprisingly, the one officer to voice misgivings about the proposal was the Judge Advocate General (the officer in charge of Military Justice), who was fully aware of the Government's intention to use troops in strikes and of the arguments for amendment. During the winter of 1919-20 the Cabinet discussed extensively the question of using soldiers to perform vital services for the community should there be a widespread or general strike. The opinion of the Judge Advocate General was sought in January 1920 as to the extent of the existing legal powers to use troops in industrial disputes and he submitted a detailed memorandum to the Cabinet.[44] It is highly significant, therefore, that he should have felt that the permanent law of the land already contained sufficient provisions to enable 'really serious attempts' to seduce soldiers to be dealt with.[45] This was not simply a statement of the existing legal provisions, but an opinion as to how far the law ought to go.

In fact the only amendment which was introduced in the House dealt with attempts to obstruct, impede or otherwise interfere with any member of His Majesty's Forces in the execution of his duty. The hostility shown in 1919 was not repeated and this provision was embodied in the Army Annual Act of 1920.

In February 1920 the Cabinet received a report entitled 'Revolutionaries and the need for legislation', from Sir Basil Thomson of the Directorate of Intelligence at the Home Office. It alluded to the success achieved by Bolshevism outside Russia by means of propaganda, and recommended new legislation to deal with 'seditious speeches and writings'. One section of the report demonstrates quite clearly the inability of Intelligence at that time to distinguish between various dissident groups. Sir Basil presented his own historical analysis of 'our own home grown revolutionary . . . since Burke's day and before'. 'At one time we know him as pro-Bonaparte, at another as pro-Communard, then as pro-Boer, pro-Indian, pro-Egyptian, and later as pro-German, in fact as pro-anything by whom it can be shown that his country was in the wrong. In moments of crisis you will find him as a passive resister, conscientious objector, or pacifist. The same persons are found in all these movements and it is natural now to find them conspiring secretly with the Soviet Government in Russia.'[46]

Appended to the report was a draft Bill which sought to render illegal the advocacy of, or the inciting to the use of *unlawful* violence as a means of overthrowing the constitutional Government of the United Kingdom. It also sought to impose penalties on persons receiving money from abroad to finance propaganda for these purposes. A Conference of Ministers was called to consider this report and another by the Home Secretary.[47] It was agreed that a committee chaired by the Lord Chancellor, Lord Birkenhead, should prepare a draft Bill for the consideration of the Cabinet.[48]

During 1920 the Lloyd George Government was presented with conclusive evidence of working class pro-Russian feeling when Trade Union and Labour Party agitation forced a change of policy and averted British involvement in Soviet-Polish hostilities.[49] By the end of the year, however, the Government had successfully armed itself for war of another kind – the inevitable show-down with the Trade Union movement. In preparation, the Government restored the emergency powers which were thought to be necessary during the Great War. The threat of a Triple Alliance strike in October 1920 in support of a miners' pay claim resulted in the Government introducing on 22 October a Bill which was enacted by the 27th, the *Emergency Powers Act 1920.* This empowers the Government, whenever action is threatened, of such a nature as to be calculated (by interference with the supply and distribution of food, water, fuel or light, or with the means of locomotion) to deprive the Community, or any substantial portion of the Community, of the essentials of life, to declare that a State of Emergency exists. This is achieved by Royal Proclamation which expires after one month but may be renewed. So long as a proclamation is in force, regulations may be made, by Order in Council under Section 2, securing the essentials of life to the community and these may confer or impose on a Secretary of State or other Government department, or any other person in Her Majesty's service or acting on Her Majesty's behalf, *such powers and duties as Her Majesty may deem necessary* for the preservation of the peace, for regulating the supply and distribution of food, water, fuel, light and other necessities, in maintaining the means of transit or locomotion, and *for any other purposes essential* to the public safety and the life of the community, and may make *such provisions* incidental to the powers aforesaid as may *appear to Her Majesty to be required* for making the exercise of these powers effective (my italics).

These regulations must be laid before Parliament immediately after they are made and they cannot continue in force after seven days unless a resolution is passed by both Houses providing for their continuance.

The Act contains provisos to the effect that nothing in it shall authorise the making of any regulation imposing any form of compulsory military service or industrial conscription; nor make it an offence for any person to take part in a strike or peacefully persuade any other person to take part in a strike; nor to alter the existing procedure in criminal cases or confer any right to punish by fine or imprisonment without trial.

The importance of the Act lies in the immensely wide powers which may be conferred on the Government by those phrases italicised above. They allow the Government to suspend practically all those civil liberties which remain and to penalise opposition to their policies. The usual practice during the 1920's was to have draft regulations prepared to be promulgated whenever necessary. These draft regulations were largely based on the DORA Regulations and included provisions relating to incitement to disaffection in the armed forces. There is no reason to suppose that this practice has been discontinued.

THE COMMUNIST PARTY, THE CAMPBELL CASE, AND THE ZINOVIEV LETTER

The formation of the Communist Party of Great Britain in 1920 provided the Government with something more tangible on which to concentrate, while the Special Branch of New Scotland Yard maintained a constant watch on communist activities and was able to provide the cabinet with increasingly detailed information.

Had the Public Order Bill which resulted from the deliberations of the committee under Lord Birkenhead, been passed into law, membership of the Communist Party would almost certainly have been illegal. The Bill encompassed the provisions of Sir Basil Thomson's draft Bill outlined above, relating to *unlawful* violence and also contained provisions relating to incitement to disaffection similar to those already discussed. Since the overthrow of capitalism and its replacement with socialism was the avowed aim of the Communist Party it could not have survived the passage of this measure. Indeed, since it did not mention the Communist Party or any other organisation the Bill was wide enough to have been used as a general purge measure.

Possession for distribution of the type of propaganda which the Bill was designed to combat was to be made an offence. The Committee realised that it would be exceptional to find positive evidence of an intention to distribute, and fear that the courts would lack sufficient power to convict induced them to reduce evidence of intention to the statistical requirement that possession of more than *three* copies of a book or leaflet 'shall be evidence of possession for the purpose of distribution'.[50]

Admittedly the presumption could be rebutted, but the Committee were seeking to shift the onus of proof onto the accused and to provide the courts with the power to convict where the evidence would not normally be sufficient to do so. Significantly, all the members of this committee were lawyers: The Lord Chancellor, Lord Birkenhead; The Home Secretary, Edward Shortt; The Attorney General, Sir Gordon Hewart (later Lord Chief Justice as Lord Hewart); The Solicitor General, Sir Ernest Pollock; and The Director of Public Prosecutions, Sir Archibald Bodkin.

Ironically, it was the Government's fear of a General Strike in April 1921 which led the Home Affairs Committee to decide not to introduce the Bill.[51] They calculated that such action might indicate undue nervousness and be regarded as a provocation. They were much more sensitive to the possibility of abuse of powers and the likelihood of opposition in the Commons than the Army Council. Opposition in the House did not directly affect the Army Council, of course, since they were not held responsible for measures introduced by the Government.

The Miners' Federation appealed for support from the Triple Alliance in their fight against the drastic wage reductions which the owners sought to impose on resuming control of the mines. On the 1 April the Government declared a State of Emergency under the Emergency Powers Act and prepared the armed forces for action. All leave was cancelled, all classes of reservists were called up, motor vehicles were requisitioned and a Special Defence Force was created for which 75,000 volunteered in ten days, when recruiting was stopped.[52] The General Strike never occurred and the Defence Force was never called into action, but the Government had shown its willingness to use all the power of the armed forces against the Trade Unions.

Despite the powers which the Executive was able to wield under the Emergency Powers Act, certain members of the Government were becoming increasingly concerned about the imminent diminution of permanent Executive powers – DORA was about to expire. The Home Secretary informed the Home Affairs Committee on 25 May that some sixty speakers had recently been prosecuted under the DORA Regullations and that convictions had been obtained in most cases. 'The Authorities would soon have no suitable means of bringing offenders to justice', he complained.[53]

The Public Order Bill having been dropped, the Army Council's attention once more focused on the Annual Army Bill and with a little prodding from Colonel Kell of MI5 to 'continue to press for attention to this serious gap in the national armoury until it is remedied', yet another amendment allowing for summary procedure to deal with attempts to cause mutiny, sedition or disaffection was proposed.[54] The Judge Advocate General, however, once more intimated that it was not clear to him why it was necessary to change the law at all, when inciting to mutiny and endeavouring to seduce from duty and allegiance were already punishable on indictment with penal servitude for life. The proposed amendment to the 1922 Bill was shelved.

As an increasing number of men joined the forces to avoid unemployment and the prospect of the forces being used against strikers and even the unemployed increased, the threat of disaffection must have appeared very real. It was unlikely that men who had known unemployment or had engaged in trade union activities would relish the thought of taking part in strike breaking or what was euphemistically known as 'preserving law and order'. The close contact between soldiers and workers in such situations lends itself to such incitements to disaffection as pleas not to shoot when ordered to do so. The Army Council, the Intelligence Services, and the Secretary of State for War, Sir L. Worthington-

Evans, all wanted to acquire the powers of the 1921 Public Order Bill which would provide penalties for this type of incitement and communist propaganda generally.[55] It was obvious, however, that they would have to bide their time and accept whatever measures any Government managed to pass through the Commons.

From 11 March 1922, during the four months of the engineers' lock-out, many members of the National Unemployed Workers' Movement were arrested, imprisoned or fined for sedition, obstruction, or acting in a manner likely to cause a breach of the peace. Police baton charges, frequently unprovoked, were not an uncommon feature of this and the following decade.[56] After one of the big battles with the police in London, an article appealing to the police not to use their batons against the unemployed appeared in *Out of Work*, a paper published by the NUWM. The editor, Mrs Thring, was arrested under the 1919 Act, on a charge of inciting to disaffection among the Metropolitan Police. She refused to pay the £10 fine imposed at Bow Street Magistrates' Court and was imprisoned for three weeks.[57] The authorities were, of course, hypersensitive about the loyalty of the police, and this charge was another malicious attack on the NUWM, which had already constituted a menace to the authorities and an embarrassment to the Government by organising the unemployed and leading them on a hunger march to London. That the principal leaders of the movement were also members of the Communist Party simply confirmed its reputation with the Government, and it was continually subjected to Special Branch surveillance and harassment.[58]

In May 1922, a Private Member's Bill, The Seditious Propaganda Bill, was introduced in the Commons by Mr Gideon Murray, MP, to prevent the importation into Great Britain of money, securities, or valuable property intended to promote revolutionary or seditious propaganda. It bore a remarkable resemblance to the 1921 Public Order Bill but in providing that a Superintendent of Police could grant a search warrant to a constable, it proposed much wider powers of search. In introducing it, Murray assured the House, 'This is quite a simple Bill, consisting of only six clauses', but despite the interest of the War Office and the approval of MI5, it was awaiting its second reading when Parliament dissolved in November 1922.[59]

When the Army Annual Bill for 1923 was introduced, the Labour Party sought to amend its provisions and, although no mention appears in the War Office files, we may assume that the proposed amendments caused some concern there. The amendments proposals included the abolition of the death penalty in the Army, the setting up of Courts of Appeal, and giving recruits the right to indicate their unwillingness to do their duty in the case of a trade dispute. The last amendment, moved by George Lansbury, was denied a second reading by 197 votes to 101.[60]

In January 1924, Ramsay Macdonald formed the first Labour Government, a minority government. The Army Council may have felt that this would, however temporarily, end their campaign for new legislation covering incitement to disaffection. No proposals for such legislation or references to the offences appear in the War Office files for the duration of the Labour administration and the Army Council was no doubt as surprised as the mass of Labour supporters by the way in which their cause was furthered during that period.

The Government opposed all the amendments to the Annual Army and Air Force Bill similar to those which had been voted for by the Party the previous year. It was announced that the Army Council had been asked to go into the whole question of service and report to the Cabinet during the ensuing year. To protests that the Army Council was out of touch with the people and the rank and file of the Army, the Secretary for War, Stephen Walsh, replied, 'it is quite wrong to refer to the Army Council as a purely military organisation, a body of obscurantists whose minds cannot possibly be open to the more democratic views that are, I suppose, specially associated with certain Hon. Members of this House'.[61]

Unfortunately, the Labour Cabinet discontinued in February 1924 the practice of circulating Special Branch Reports as Cabinet Papers. These reports were much more comprehensive than those which had come from the Directorate of Intelligence at the Home Office and had included under the title 'Revolutionary Organisations in the United Kingdom', such subheadings as 'The Daily Herald', 'The Coalminers' and 'The Scottish Labour College'.[62] The Special Branch informed the Cabinet in January that the decision of the Labour Party to accept Communists as individual members subject to certain conditions had caused great satisfaction in Communist circles: instructions had been issued by the Political Bureau to the effect that all Communists were to secure membership of the Labour Party 'without any display of ostentation' within the next month or so, the intention apparently being to get Communist MPs via the Labour ticket.[63] This decision was to be overturned at the Labour Party Conference of that year, but in the meantime a close watch was kept on Communist activities. The

Home Secretary, Arthur Henderson, was able to quote freely from the private correspondence of leading members of the Communist Party, while an Industrial Unrest Committee was set up to investigate the part played by Communists in industrial unrest.[64] Sidney Webb, President of the Board of Trade in that Government, later disclosed that the Home Secretary reported weekly to the Prime Minister but that these reports were not published and were even with-held from the Cabinet 'deliberately in order not to make too much out of what was really a very insignificant movement'.[65]

Such was the attitude of the Government to strikes that Henderson refused to reinstate the men who had been dismissed from the Police Force in 1919, on the ground that they had rejected 'constitutional methods' in engineering the strike against the institution of the Federation, which since then had stood consistently for such constitutional methods.[66] The Government's preparedness to use troops in industrial disputes came as a great shock to the Labour movement, but it was only after considerable discussion that the Cabinet decided to invoke the Emergency Powers Act in a transport strike in London. They had originally intended to use naval ratings to keep power stations in operation *without issuing a Proclamation of a State of Emergency,*[67] only after the Lord Advocate, H.P. Mitchell, advised that the use of the Act would avoid any possibility of illegality in the employment of members of the forces did the Cabinet decide on such a step.[68]

In the face of such a volte-face from previous Labour policies, it was inevitable that 'Don't Shoot' exhortations to soldiers would reappear in print. Events were to show, however, that not all members of the Government were prepared for such propaganda.

On 25 July 1924, the Communist *Workers' Weekly* published such an appeal to soldiers, exhorting them to 'let it be known that neither in the class war nor in the military war will you turn your guns on your fellow workers'. Members of the Armed Forces were urged to form committees in every barracks, aerodrome and ship, which would refuse to go to war or shoot workers during industrial disputes but instead join with the workers to smash capitalism. Such appeals were not uncommon, but, as Leslie Macfarlane points out, 'there was something faintly ludicrous in the Communist Party issuing a call of this nature when it would probably have found it hard to muster a couple of dozen members in the whole of the Armed Forces'.[69]

On 6 August, an announcement in the House confirmed the decision to prosecute J.R. Campbell, the editor of *Workers' Weekly* under the

Incitement to Mutiny Act. Labour back benchers were horrified and their subsequent hounding of the Attorney General, Sir Patrick Hastings, brought the full significance of the proposed prosecution to his attention. One member declared that if sentiments such as those in the article were to become cause for prosecution, the Government would find half its party in the dock.[70]

The Communist Party sent a letter to all Labour MPs declaring that Campbell, as temporary editor, was not responsible for the article, which in any case merely deplored the use of the armed forces in industrial disputes. The Attorney General had meanwhile obtained information from James Maxton, Chairman of the Independent Labour Party, to the effect that Campbell was 'a man of excellent character with an admirable military record', who 'had had both feet blown off fighting for his King and Country' – this latter was, in fact, untrue.[71] Treasury Counsel was thus able to justify the Government's withdrawal of the prosecution on 13 August, and that might have concluded the grand farce which had taken place behind the scenes, had the Communist Party not firmly reiterated their involvement in the proceedings. By so doing, they played right into the hands of the Tories by presenting them with the 'evidence' they longed for. Ignoring the contents of their circular letter, they immediately admitted that Campbell was a member of the Political Bureau of the Party, asserted that the article was deliberately an appeal to soldiers to refuse to fight in all cases, and claimed that it was owing to the strength of the British Communist Party and its influence on the Parliamentary Labour Party that the left wing of the PLP had compelled the Cabinet to order the prosecution to be withdrawn.[72] The Conservatives were able to raise the cry of political interference with the course of justice and they tabled a motion of censure when Parliament met at the end of September.

No-one in the Cabinet was really sure how the prosecution had been authorised or who was responsible for authorising it. It was discussed at a Cabinet meeting on 6 August,[73] and from notes taken by Thomas Jones, Assistant Secretary to the Cabinet, it appears that the Attorney General had advised prosecution and that documents had passed from the Director of Public Prosecutions to the Army Council, then to the Home Office and back to the DPP. The assistant DPP was quite adamant that the Home Secretary had consented to prosecution, but Henderson denied this and the Attorney General explained that there had been an ambiguity in the minute from the Home Secretary. Macdonald disingenuously claimed that his first source of information on the matter had been a newspaper article.[74]

Hastings accepted full responsibility for proceeding with the case and recommended continuation of the prosecution. He did however outline the possible justifications for withdrawal and Cabinet Conclusion 48 (24) 5 (6) states that this course was to be adopted. After the prosecution had been withdrawn Macdonald challenged the accuracy of this conclusion and insisted that Hankey, Secretary to the Cabinet, should file Jones' notes with the Cabinet minutes.

In answer to a private notice Question on 30 September, the Prime Minister claimed that he had not been consulted on the institution of proceedings or on their subsequent withdrawal. His later statement that, in saying this, he 'had gone a little further than I ought to have done', did not improve matters. The Tories decided to support a Liberal motion demanding a Select Committee of Investigation but the Cabinet had already agreed that this was to be regarded as a motion of censure and that the Prime Minister should ask for a dissolution if it were carried. They also rejected the course advocated by the Attorney General, of offering some less partisan form of alternative inquiry by a Royal Commission, the judicial committee of the Privy Council or a Judge.[75] The Government was defeated by 304 to 191 votes.

The notion of non-interference of the Executive in the institution of criminal proceedings, and hence the refusal publicly to acknowledge prosecutions as political, is a stock myth of the British Constitution. It is a myth which the Macdonald Government, had they wished, could have done much to expose. The hypocrisy of a number of former Ministers would not have been difficult to uncover. Sir Douglas Hogg, soon to be Attorney General and later Lord Chancellor, admitted to D.N. Pritt (later a Labour MP) that they 'wanted to get rid of these dreadful people on any excuse, however bad', while Asquith stated privately that any Attorney General who did not withdraw a prosecution when ordered by his Prime Minister to do so would be out of a job next morning.[76]

The defeat of the Labour Government over the Campbell case avoided defeat on the question of the General and Commercial Treaty which it had signed with Russia.[77] Both affairs, however, raised doubts about the relationship between the Labour Party and Communism, and the publication, just before polling day, of a letter allegedly from Zinoviev, president of the Third International, to the British Communist Party, linking support of the Treaty with plans for class war in Great Britain, settled those doubts, at least in the minds of ardent anti-Bolsheviks. The new Baldwin Government was convinced of the authenticity of the letter, although Austen Chamberlain refused to divulge the evidence, stating merely that the essence of a secret service is that it is secret.[78]

For present purposes the importance of the so-called Zinoviev Letter lies not in whether it was a forgery but in the instructions it contained and the fact that the Government believed they hailed from the Third International. One instruction related to the spread of revolutionary disaffection in the Army by the creation of Communist Cells. There was nothing revelatory in this so far as the War Office was concerned: Sir Basil Thomson had quoted instructions to this effect purporting to come from the Third International as early as 1921.[79] The reference to the 'military section of the British Communist Party' was new, because it did not exist, and this together with the comprehensive nature of the instructions and the inclusion of such phrases as 'the future directors of the British Red Army' undoubtedly unnerved the military authorities. 'By the end of 1924', Pelling observes, 'the British Communist Party could claim to have had some influence on the course of national history. But this was by courtesy of the Conservatives and their press, and not through any positive influence of its own.[80]

Incitement to Disaffection and the Armed Forces 1924-31

THE 'WORKERS' WEEKLY' PROSECUTIONS

Early in December 1924, the Baldwin Cabinet decided that an inquiry into the proceedings of the Campbell case would no longer be desirable or in the public interest.[81] They also decided to revoke a decision of the Labour Cabinet (48 [24] 5) to the effect that no public prosecution of a political character should be undertaken without the prior consent of the Cabinet being obtained. On 13 December this was intimated to the Commons by the Prime Minister in response to a question whether an inquiry was to be held on the Campbell case. The Home Secretary, the obscurantist William Joynson Hicks, was still sufficiently concerned about the possible repercussions of that case to prepare a Cabinet memorandum entitled 'The Institution of Political Prosecutions'.[82] He explained that the practice which had been followed for more than forty years with entirely satisfactory results allowed the Attorney General and the DPP complete autonomy so far as concerned prosecutions involving no question of public security or state interest. Where a prosecution might involve any consideration of public security or any interest of state it was the bounden duty of those officers, before deciding upon a prosecution, to ascertain the views of the Ministerial Department best qualified to pronounce upon the public interest involved – 'The Department in ordinary political cases being the Home Office'.[83] In the light of subsequent events it would not be unjust to suggest that Hicks' concern here was not to present a definitive statement of the Constitutional position of the Attorney General and the DPP, but to ensure that he, as Home Secretary, would not be denied the right to promote proceedings against the communists.

He drew attention to several cases referred to in the minutes of the War Cabinet, the most remarkable of which had been engineered at a conference held at 10 Downing Street on 17 May 1917. The Prime Minister, Lloyd George, the Attorney General, Sir F.E. Smith, and the DPP, Sir Charles Mathews, among others, had decided that eight or ten persons should be chosen against whom there was sufficient evidence to warrant proceedings for inciting strikes in the engineering trade. Instructions had been given that the accused should be furnished with full statements of the charges against them, that applications for bail should not be opposed, that the case for the Crown should be presented in detail to give the public an opinion on its merits, and that the trial should be by jury at the Old Bailey. Eight men were accordingly arrested but the prosecution was dropped upon their giving an undertaking to adhere to an agreement arrived at on 19 May between the Ministry of Munitions and the Executive Council of the Amalgamated Society of Engineers. Nothing could demonstrate more conclusively the extent to which the executive can, did and perhaps does manipulate the institution of proceedings to further its own political causes. Hicks, though, seemed oblivious of his own inconsistency when justifying the attack on Hastings on the ground that the latter had withdrawn the prosecution of Campbell after the Executive had intervened, 'not upon any grounds of *public interest* but upon purely party grounds and in deference to pressure exerted by a section of their supporters whose political views and objects can hardly be distinguished from those of the proprietors of the *Workers' Weekly* and the author of the "Open Letter".'[84] The public did not have long to wait for Hicks to demonstrate what was in their interest.

Early in July 1925 Communist notices appeared on barracks walls at Aldershot. The Home Office immediately requested to be informed of any reports of 'Bolshevist propaganda' at military centres.[85] At the end of the month MI5 obtained information that the Communist Party (District Party Committee Propaganda Dept.) had arranged for distribution of stickers, posters, and had printed five-minute speeches for their Anti-War Week from 2-9 August.[86] A War Office circular was promptly dispatched to Commanding Officers of District Commands requesting details of propaganda and requiring them to forward any leaflets or other evidence which had come into their hands. Leaflets which had been torn from walls were hastily pieced together and sent, complete with brick and plaster specimens to the War Office, where the information that one sticker had been found on the Order Board of a Post at Buckingham Palace caused considerable consternation.[87]

The stickers which the War Office found so objectionable carried such messages as:

'A General lifts 75/9d a day. A private gets 2/9d. What about a bit of the top? Immediate increase for the rank and file.'

'Why should Officers get twice as much leave as us and be able to knock about in civvies? A free pass every weekend when not on duty.'

'The Bosses want lower wages and longer hours when the workers strike; fight with them, not against them.'

Perhaps the most objectionable poster so far as the authorities were concerned was one entitled 'The Communist Programme for the Forces'. It set out fourteen points which the Communist Party was said to stand for. They were:

1 Formation of soldiers and sailors committees.
2 The right to join political parties and attend meetings.
3 The right to join trade unions.
4 No troops to be used against strikers.
5 Immediate pay increase for the rank and file.

6 Equal leave for men and officers.
7 The right to wear civvies on leave.
8 Shorter Service Periods and an eight-hour day.
9 Full trade union rates for soldiers in Government work-shops.
10 Men's Committees to control rations etc.
11 No compulsory church parades.
12 Increased pensions for widows and orphans.
13 Boys not to be sent on active service.
14 The abolition of all reserves.

A Special Branch Report of 13 August added to the general alarm by informing the Army Council that a letter, dated 25 July, headed 'Executive Committee of Communist International, Anglo-American Section', and addressed to the Central Committee of the British Communist Party, had exhorted the latter to 'start preparing Literature and Workers for the troops. Let the general strike movement serve to encourage the dissatisfaction of the oppressed soldiers and open their eyes to the nature of the class struggle'.[88] Whether that letter was genuine or even existed, is dubious, but it is worth noting that all the Intelligence Services, and the Special Branch, were intent on gaining new powers to deal with Communist propaganda. They frequently took the opportunity to exaggerate or even invent the information or evidence which they included in their reports to the Cabinet. Their job was to provide information and their sources were informers and *agents provocateurs,* who were also paid to deliver the goods.

The sense of utter frustration with the inadequacy of the existing legislation is evident in the details of the only prosecutions reported on account of the stickers. Three men were charged with defacing a wall without consent and fined forty shillings.[89] The general feeling of the Army Council now was that a new Bill would be better than an amendment to the Army and Air Force Annual Bill, but that it should extend to actions likely to prejudice recruiting. MI5 were also against an amendment 'because it would have no beneficial effect for the Navy, Police or Civil Service, all of which are equally in need of protection'.[90] This was the earliest hint that it was not just the armed forces which needed to be isolated from political discussion, and it was to be more fully discussed at a later stage.

The *Workers' Weekly* of 7 August once again carried a leader suggesting that soldiers and sailors must be urged not to use their weapons against the working class and the edition of 14 August claimed that

14,000 copies of a circular which reproduced the actual words of the Campbell 'Don't Shoot' letter had been distributed, mainly through factory newspapers. They were also sent 'as enclosures to friends and relations in the Forces'.

At a Home Office Conference on 21 August, the Attorney-General, Sir Douglas Hogg, Hicks and representatives of the Service Departments discussed the question of proceedings.[91] Hogg believed that only one sticker was probably seditious, but he was not prepared to say that a jury would find it so. He suggested that if more leeway were given to the Communist Party they would go further and put themselves more clearly within the law; proceedings would then be possible against leading members and there would be greater certainty of convincing a jury and of securing the support of public opinion. This was exactly what happened. On 7 October, Hicks gave the Cabinet particulars of arrangements he had made with the Attorney-General and the DPP for keeping under observation the activities and speeches of Communists with a view to action 'at the proper time'.[92] Six days later Sir Douglas Hogg presented to the Cabinet a Memorandum entitled 'The present law in regard to sedition and strikes'.[93] This considered two branches of the law: the power of the state to punish or prevent the preaching of revolutionary doctrine which might prevent any chance of a *peaceful settlement,* and the limits within which a general strike in support of the miners' demands was permissable. Not surprisingly the first aspect of the law which Sir Douglas considered was the width of the 1797 Act and the question of 'Communist attempts to prevent the armed forces from carrying out their duties in the event of a strike'. His discussion of the type of conduct which is not covered by that Act demonstrates in the clearest possible manner the absolute control which the Executive felt they had a right to exercise over members of the forces: 'It is plain that great discontent might easily be stirred up in the forces without coming within the provisions of this law, for example, suggestions to the rank and file that they ought to have more pay, more privileges and more freedom, even if couched in very offensive language would seem not to be criminal unless they were accompanied by incitement to refuse to obey orders'. Hogg felt that much of the law was 'archaic' in that it did not provide sufficient power to deal with present problems. He admitted that it was not easy to decide whether any particular language does or does not amount to sedition and observed that 'the necessity of a jury trial involves very considerable delay before a conviction can be obtained'. Sensitive to public opinion, however, the Attorney-General warned the Cabinet that it is essential 'to avoid any undue interference with the liberty of speech: and any proposal which avoids trial by jury is bound to be very jealously scrutinised'. This statement appears incongruous only if one assumes, as the Attorney-General did not, that liberty of speech extends to Communists and to members of the armed forces.

It is interesting to note in passing that in this memorandum can also be seen the embryonic stage of the Trades Disputes Act of 1927. The Attorney-General had no doubt about the legality of a general strike under existing law.

The Cabinet was informed at the same meeting that evidence was available to justify the arrest and prosecution of nine leading British Communists. The Attorney-General wanted them arrested immediately, but before a final decision was taken he wished to consult the Cabinet as to whether there were any factors in the national or industrial situation which rendered the prosecutions undesirable. The Cabinet duly consented.[94]

Following raids on the headquarters of the Communist Party, the National Minority Movement, and on various private houses, twelve Executive members of the Party, including J.R. Campbell, were arrested on 14 October 1925.[95] They were charged with conspiring, since 1 January 1924, to utter and publish seditious libels; to incite persons to commit breaches of the Incitement to Mutiny Act 1797; and to endeavour to seduce from their duty persons serving in His Majesty's forces to whom might come certain publications, to wit the *Workers' Weekly* and others, and to incite them to mutiny.

Such was the joy of the Home Secretary, Hicks, that he immediately indulged in what even *The Times* described as 'a most improper whoop over the arrest of the still unconvicted Communists', informing a meeting in his constituency that warrants had been applied for against a certain number of 'notorious Communists' and that several of them were already in custody. 'When this trial is over', he said, 'those of you who are Communists will be ashamed of yourselves.' Commenting on this, D.N. Pritt wrote, 'Any lawyer should have known that such an observation was grossly improper, but Joynson Hicks, although a lawyer, was not conspicuous for his discretion or intelligence.'[96]

Prosecuting Counsel on 24 October at the Police Court was Sir Travers Humphreys, Treasury Counsel, who had withdrawn the Campbell prosecution the year before. The attitude of the Government was immediately apparent when in his opening speech he attempted to achieve by legal argument what the Executive had so far failed to achieve in legislation. His basic thesis was that the Communist Party of Great Britain and the Young Communist League were illegal organisations and that the accused were 'all engaged in an illegal conspiracy, preaching the doctrines of what they call Communism. All persons who disseminate either by word of mouth or by published writings the doctrines which these persons call Communism are liable to be prosecuted for one or other of the branches of what is commonly called sedition – uttering seditious words or publishing seditious libels. Communism hails from Russia.' He submitted that Communism was illegal because it involved three things: the overthrow of the constituted Government of the country and the established forms of government by force; the creation of antagonism between different classes of His Majesty's subjects – class war; the seducing from their allegiance of the armed forces of the Crown.

While, as we have seen, the legal authorities did believe that a considerable amount of Communist propaganda was seditious and actionable, they were not prepared to institute proceedings on a large scale and they would certainly not have prosecuted Communists simply because they were members of the Party. There was really no legal justification for Counsel's submission that the Communist party itself was an illegal organisation, whatever 'crimes' were committed in the name of Communism. Presumably this was simply a public show of force in the hope of frightening off the less committed propagandists. The assertion of illegality may well have influenced Sir John Simon in the development of his more famous though equally inaccurate thesis of the illegality of a General Strike.

The trial lasted for three weeks at the Old Bailey. The accuseds' public speeches, literature of the Party, and the *Workers' Weekly* were extensively quoted by the Attorney-General to prove that they were preparing for struggle against the ruling class in defence of the miners. The charge of Incitement to Mutiny was made on the ground that in their speeches and press they had urged that in the event of a general strike and the soldiers being called upon to use arms against the workers, they should remember their working class origin, and be ready not to shoot their own brothers. Crown evidence did not substantiate the charge that the Party was an illegal organisation, but the accused made good use of the opportunity to expose what they saw as the class nature of the proceedings. Like Tom Mann in 1912 they made much of the contrast between their own persecution and the treatment of

Carson (by now a Judge in the House of Lords), Smith (Secretary for India), and others. When one of the accused, Tom Bell, cross-examined a witness at the Police Court with regard to what he called 'the Ulster business' the magistrate pointed out that it was not necessary to go back so far as that. Bell retorted, 'I submit that as we have gone back to 1797, I am entitled to go back to 1911.'[97]

The accused were duly convicted on all three charges and five of them were sentenced to one year's imprisonment on each charge to run concurrently. The remaining seven then had the proposition put to them by Mr Justice Rigby Swift, that if they would renounce Communism and give a declaration to the effect that they would not engage in any further political activities similar to those which formed the basis of the charges, they could go free. They all refused and were sentenced to six months imprisonment. It is difficult to believe that this astonishing proposition represented a spontaneous effusion of justice or leniency. There is a temptation to imagine that it was a naive ploy designed to split the leadership of the Party.

On a vote of censure moved on the Government for having instituted the above prosecution, Hicks had brought to his attention a speech which he had made on 6 December 1913. 'The people of Ulster,' he had said, 'have behind them the Unionist Party. Behind them is the Lord God of Battles. In his name and your name I say to the Prime Minister. "Let your armies and batteries fire. Fire if you dare. Fire and be damned!".' He stated that he regretted having made the speech and added, 'I at all events was not involved in any of the activities.' The Lords Carson and Birkenhead were safely in the House of Lords.

Whether the 1925 prosecution was, as many thought at the time, a deliberate preparation for the coming General Strike or simply another round in the anti-communist campaign, five of the accused were safely out of the way during that strike and were not released until 10 September 1926. By that time the Home Office had 'selected for publication as being of general public interest' one hundred and sixty pages of material from the 'mass of documents . . . seized at the headquarters of the Communist Party of Great Britain . . . and of the National Minority Movement . . . and at other addresses.'[98] The legality of such seizure was doubtful, but the Home Office were obviously confident that they had a right to publish.

While the Communists were being tried, a Cabinet Committee was considering the Attorney-General's memorandum and the case for new 'Public Order' legislation.[99] They reported to the Cabinet on 26 March

1926 that they did not propose any legislation should be introduced at present but that it should be brought forward if and when an emergency arose and offered a favourable opportunity.[100] The committee had learned at least one lesson from the Communists' trial, that the offender is given a free advertisement in a trial at Assizes. Summary procedure would be much more expedient in such cases, they thought, especially since 'the presence in the jury of one person who is in sympathy with the offender's views . . . may render the trial abortive.' Whereas the Attorney-General had paid lip service to freedom of speech, the Committee, which included the Attorney-General and the Home Secretary, reported 'it is essential to avoid, so far as possible, the imputation that legislation is designed unduly to interfere with freedom of speech.'[101]

Just as the Home Affairs Committee in 1921 had decided not to introduce the Public Order Bill because of the industrial situation, this committee was afraid that the introduction of their Bill might 'precipitate an industrial crisis.'[102]

The War Office was again concerned about propaganda leaflets early in 1926, but the DPP, who had been sent copies of a Communist Party Pamphlet entitled 'The Soldiers' Conscience', thought that although it was 'of an insidious character', it did not form 'a suitable subject for criminal proceedings'. Despite this, the DPP suggested that Commanding Officers in barracks should exercise all vigilance to discover and if possible confiscate copies circulating amongst or in the possession of soldiers. Such an instruction, to 'seize and destroy', was sent on 16 March by the War Office to all Commands and Districts.[103] It is obvious then, if it were ever in doubt, that in the absence of legal power of control over the activities of civilians, the military authorities simply assumed the right to censor the reading material of members of the forces. Several men were removed from army units in Aldershot in the period between 1925 and 1929 for 'communistic activities', but the Commander in Chief of the Aldershot Command was apparently satisfied that as a general rule 'communistic literature' had no effect on the troops, and in fact was treated by them as a joke. However, 'in certain cases where there are one or more communists in a unit, the literature is a danger as it forms a basis for argument and is a means of spreading propaganda'.[104] It is worth remembering that until 1951 there was no appeal from the decision of a Court Martial to a civil court and when the Court Martial Appeal Court was set up in that year it was soon apparent that the strict rules of procedure and evidence applied in the civil courts played no part in the Court Martial.[105]

On 30 April 1926 the King signed a Proclamation of a State of Emergency under the Emergency Powers Act of 1920. As on the two previous occasions when this had happened, all leave in the Army was cancelled. This time troops were moved to Lancashire, Wales and Scotland, where they were 'placed at the disposal of the police, to be called upon only in emergency to preserve public order'.[106] Preserving public order, of course, included intimidating pickets and protecting strike breakers as well as parading in armoured cars in the London Docks area, and the Government announced on 7 May that any action which the Armed Forces took 'in an honest endeavour to aid the civil power' would be fully supported by the Government.[107] This was tantamount to giving them a free hand, but what violence did occur at the hands of the military did not escalate. Several police baton charges did take place, but such police violence was far from being a peculiarity of this strike.

The Communist Party was taken by surprise when the strike actually began, but it is surprising, especially in view of the invoking of the 1920 Act to provide the Executive with the vast discretionary powers deemed necessary to smash the enemy, that propaganda distribution amongst the Forces appears to have slackened, if not actually ground to a halt, around March 1926. Certainly there is no mention of any such propaganda in the War Office files relating to the later months of that year or during 1927. Communist Party membership received a sharp boost in 1926; according to Pelling it had reached 6,000 before the strike, but by October it had risen to 10,730, the great majority of the new recruits being miners. The boom was short lived, however, and by October 1927 the total membership was down to 7,377 and was falling rapidly.[108]

There was also a respite in 1926/27 in the endeavours to amend the law relating to seditious propaganda. No doubt the authorities had other problems to deal with, but in this area it turned out to be a lull before a storm. That lull was extended by a prosecution in June 1928 under the Scottish Common Law of Sedition. Four Blantyre miners were found guilty by a jury, of acting in concert in circulating seditious pamphlets among four of twenty two soldiers mentioned in the indictment. It was alleged that circulation of the pamphlet, which advocated trade unionism in the forces, was 'calculated to excite disaffection, commotion, and resistance to lawful authority among His Majesty's lieges, and particularly among His Majesty's Forces'. The pamphlet opened by asking 'What about Civvies?' and recommended the soldiers in the ranks to 'make doddering old Commanding Officers sit up' if they refused to apply the permissive order of the War Office whereby soldiers could wear civilian clothes when off duty. Each of the accused was sentenced to one month's imprisonment.[109] The military authorities did not doubt that such prosecutions had a salutary effect; conviction of these four miners was accepted as the reason why no fresh pamphlets of any kind were seen in the UK for nearly a year.[110] This and the knowledge that in the existing stage of English law it would be impossible to obtain a conviction for the same offence added force to the arguments for amendment.

THE INVERGORDON MUTINY

The year 1929 witnessed a dramatic intensification both of communist leafletting of barracks and of corresponding attempts to amend the law to deal with them. The appropriate Ministers in the 1929 Labour Government did not seek to further the cause with the same fervour as their predecessors but there was no decisive change of attitude.

The appearance at military establishments throughout the Country and in the Atlantic Fleet of several pamphlets which purported to be written wholly or partly by serving soldiers, the Revolutionary Group of British Soldiers, and the first edition in September 1929 of *The Soldiers' Voice*, purporting to be the organ of Communists in the forces apparently confirmed the worst fears of the Army Council – that the Armed Forces had been infiltrated by Communists. The conviction of two distributors of *The Soldiers' Voice* under a bye-law, although prompting the local organiser of the Party to stop circulation of several thousand copies which had been sent to Manchester for distribution amongst soldiers in Lancashire, did little to ease the Army Council's frustration that no action was being taken against propagandists. They were sure that the circulation of seditious or subversive propaganda was now, perhaps for the first time, to be regarded as actually dangerous.[111] The news that the Home Secretary, J.R. Clynes, had no objection to action being taken against persons who had thrown leaflets over barrack walls raised a glimmer of hope, which was dampened by the refusal of the DPP to prosecute for sedition or incitement to mutiny as 'the procedure was complicated, expensive and out of all proportion to the gravity of the offence'.[112] His suggestion was that a short Act should be passed to enable the police to arrest without a warrant and place offenders before a magistrate who could deal with them summarily. This obviously appealed to the Army Council, who still regarded the 1921 Public Order Bill as their panacea. Sensitive to the acutely controversial nature of such a Bill, however, the Home Secretary was aware that its introduction by a Labour Government, the previous Government having decided against it, might produce a situation of considerable embarassment. In stating 'it could hardly be contended that the Communist menace has become more serious of late', the Home Office denied the justification, which the War Office had just offered, for such a measure.[113] It is astonishing that Clynes was prepared to support an amendment to the Annual Army and Air Force Bill on the ground that this would not be regarded as placing restrictions upon the individual's liberty of expression, while a general Bill would. Naturally, the Army Council were only too willing to take advantage of the Home Secretary's support, but the Secretary for War, T. Shaw, perhaps more mindful than Clynes of the 1923 and 1924 debates on the Annual Bill, 'regretted' that he regarded the political considerations as overriding the military considerations and could not contemplate legislation through the medium of the annual Act for 1930.[114] These contrasting opinions created a stalemate which lasted throughout the life of the Labour Government.

Nevertheless, prosecutions of anti-militarists continued during the years 1929-31. In 1930, at least four Communists received sentences under the Incitement to Mutiny Act 1797. One of them, A.J. Thomas, received eighteen months imprisonment for handing out leaflets at Aldershot. During the ensuing protests, four members of the Workers Press, which ran the Communist *Daily Worker,* were gaoled for contempt of court in denouncing the trial. Early in 1931, following a mutiny on board HMS *Lucia* at Plymouth over cuts in Christmas leave, extra Sunday duties, and fierce ship disclipine, further arrests were made. A Communist called Fairman was charged under the 1797 Act as a result of a speech made in Bristol on 9 February. Newspaper reports of his case make no mention of servicemen in the audience, and it may have been this factor which led to Fairman receiving the relatively lenient sentence of twelve months binding over, although he was found guilty. His case is significant, however, for being based on a speech, not on a document.[115]

In Scotland, where in 1930 a Dundee Communist, Duncan Butchart, had received a five months sentence for incitement to mutiny, a nineteen-year-old Communist, John Gollan (later to be the General Secretary of the CPGB from 1956-75), was arrested on 10 May 1931 charged with incitement to mutiny for handing out copies of *The Soldiers' Voice*. The charges against Gollan arose from an anti-recruitment campaign conducted by Edinburgh Communists at a Territorial review in the city. On 20 July, the jury found Gollan not guilty of incitement to mutiny, but guilty of the subsidiary common law charge of causing disaffection. The sheriff sentenced him to six months imprisonment for 'inciting soldiers to disaffection'. The *Daily Worker*, whose editorial on the case was this time heavily censored by the printers, exclaimed: 'John Gollan is in a prison cell for attempting to exercise the right of free speech'.[116]

Immediately after the Labour Government fell in August 1931 and the so-called National Government under Macdonald was formed, drastic economy cuts were made in unemployment benefits and in the salaries of various state employees. Although these averaged around 10%, the actual cut in the case of the Navy ranged as high as 25% for some Able-Bodied Seamen.[117] This inevitably caused considerable dissatisfaction, especially among married men, who had married confident in the belief, based on the pronouncements of previous Governments, that their pay would not be reduced. Many of them had rented houses, bought furniture on hire-purchase, entered into insurances and so forth. They now foresaw the impossibility of meeting these financial obligations. Moreover, the problem was greatly exacerbated by the early date at which the cuts were to take effect – 1 October. On 13 and 14 September, just after the cuts had been announced and the sailors had read about them in the newspapers, discussions took place in the large Navy canteen at Invergordon, where most of the ships of the Atlantic Fleet were engaged in training exercises. On 15 September, 12,000 men refused to obey orders to fall in for work and the 'Invergordon Mutiny' hit the headlines.[118] On the following day, the Cabinet refused as unacceptable the recommendation of the Board of the Admiralty that the pay reductions be deferred for a month to allow time for review. The Cabinet was fearful of the consequences which any concession would have on the whole scheme of 'Government economies', especially when it might be represented as a surrender to force.[119] By 21 November, they had come to the conclusion that the simplest way of removing grievances was to limit reductions for teachers, the police and the three defence services to not more than 10% and a statement to this effect was made by the Prime Minister. Mowat calculates that the proposed reductions in Navy pay and pensions would, at best, have produced little over £1½ million in savings; 'over this trifle, Britain had its "mutiny" and lost the gold standard'.[120]

It is a mistake to consider the outbreak in the Navy as confined to the Home Fleet at Invergordon. A naval correspondent, writing in *The New Statesmen* of 26 May 1934, claimed that had it not been for the prompt action of the Governor-General of Hong Kong, on the advice of the Commander-in-Chief, in closing down all unauthorised wireless communications from the island, a telegram expressing the unanimous backing of the China Fleet would have reached the *Valiant* at Invergordon. There was also at least one incident on board the HMS *Delhi* in the West Indies, when seamen and mariners refused to turn to.[121]

However, the publicity was confined to Invergordon and from there thirty-six 'ringleaders' were dismissed without charges being brought against them. That was far from being an end of the matter. The Cabinet was informed on 21 September by the First Lord of the Admiralty, Sir Austen Chamberlain, that the Intelligence Services, including MI5, were convinced trouble was going to erupt the following week in Plymouth and Portsmouth when the ships from Invergordon arrived there.[122] The only trouble which did occur seems to have been manufactured by those Services, but after all the fuss which had been made about Communist propaganda and the rising menace of Communism, the authorities were not easily convinced that the Mutiny had been a spontaneous eruption organised by the men themselves. In fact, they were not convinced at all. It was not just that it suited the Government to claim that Communist propaganda had been a major cause – admittedly a scapegoat was as useful to the Executive as it had been in 1797 – but it was utterly beyond their conception that members of the Royal Navy could or would hatch such a plot without external influence. If evidence of that was not available, it had to be manufactured.

It is true, as Pelling suggests, that it suited the Communists to play up the credit that this offered them.[123] The *Daily Worker*, the successor of the *Workers' Weekly*, responded immediately to news of the Mutiny. On 17 September, it appealed to all sailors to join the 'no cuts' fight and argued that the sailors being confined to their ships would not 'prevent the movement spreading through the Navy and stretching out to the Army and Air Force'. The following day it informed readers that the ships of the Atlantic Fleet were soon to arrive at Davenport, Portsmouth, Chatham and Sheerness and urged that the crews 'be greeted by workers and helped to raise in those ports precisely those questions which were raised at Invergordon'.

The Special Branch were not slow to act and, true to form, searched the *Daily Worker* offices without a warrant.[124] When they returned, however, the only person they could find to arrest was W.T. Wilkinson, Managing Director of Utopia Press Ltd., printers of the paper. He was charged under Section 1 of the 1797 Act and further charges were later added of conspiring with others responsible for the production of the paper to contravene that Act, and to invite other persons to do so.[125] In answer to the defence submission that, as Managing Director of the printing firm, Wilkinson could not be held responsible for the paper's contents, counsel for the Crown submitted that where Incitement to Mutiny is in printed form the printer is equally responsible and perhaps more so than the person who prepares the matter for publication, since without his help and co-operation the incitement would not be so widespread. What could better demonstrate the determination to stamp out undesirable political propaganda? Yet, in his summing up, Mr Justice Hawkes insisted that it was essential that it should be stated that there was 'no law in the country to prevent political propaganda'.[126] Wilkinson was found guilty on both counts under Section 1 of the Act, but no evidence was brought on the conspiracy charges. The judge left no doubt that he understood the effect of the Court action, even if he would not have accepted that it was the very reason for the prosecution. 'I shall follow my usual practice of sending you to the second division, bearing in mind your age (68) and also bearing in mind that, I suppose, this will largely smash the business of Utopia Press Ltd.[127] Wilkinson was sentenced to nine months imprisonment and the printing profession received another sharp reminder that it was responsible in law for the material it printed.

Only one of Wilkinson's fellow 'conspirators', Frank Patterson, was subsequently brought to trial. After Crown Counsel had reminded the jury that 'there is no question of political views in this case', and that 'people are entitled to put forward their political views, to urge their political claims, in a proper way', Patterson was found guilty and Mr Justice Humphreys sentenced him to two years hard labour.[128] Mr Justice Humphreys was formerly Sir Travers Humphreys, Treasury Counsel, propounder of the thesis of the illegality of the Communist Party in the 1925 Trial.

Sir Percival Clarke, prosecuting in these cases, had stressed that it was not suggested that those responsible for the publication were responsible for the Navy unrest over pay cuts. Such a statement could of course be used to imply that there was considerable doubt, but in any case there is evidence that the Admiralty and the Security Services were at that time endeavouring to find evidence of just such an involvement.

The one prosecution which did take place after this investigation is discussed in Wincott's book, but he obviously was not aware of all the facts which came out at the trial. He does, though, indicate other instances of 'a massive search for hidden agitators, secret societies and all sorts of non-existent seditious groups that could never have found a square inch of fertile ground in the Royal Navy', including a particularly pathetic attempt to ensnare him.[129]

A man called Hutchings met a sailor named Bateman on 23 September 1931, in a Portsmouth fish and chip shop just after the latter had arrived from Invergordon. Hutchings represented himself as a journalist in search of a story and bought Bateman fish and chips and drinks for the rest of the night. Bateman introduced Hutchings to a fellow sailor named Bousfield, at which point Hutchings revealed that he was 'a member of the Third International' and told them that he wanted the sailors to come out on strike. The two naval men misrepresented to Hutchings that they had taken prominent parts in the Invergordon troubles and Hutchings, not to be outdone, informed them that he was a leading communist and offered Bousfield £100 and a good job in Russia if he would co-operate in starting another sailors' strike.[130] While Bousfield, whom Wincott claims had been an informer at Invergordon, reported to his Commanding Officer and agreed to act under instructions, Hutchings went to London and called on William Shepherd, a trade union official and member of the staff of the *Daily Worker*. He enquired whether Shepherd would like to meet one of the Invergordon leaders and introduced him to Bousfield, who had now also come to London. It was decided that Bousfield should draft a pamphlet to be circulated among sailors, and that he, Bateman and a sailor named Smithson, whom they invented, would circulate them in certain ships. Shepherd agreed to get the pamphlet printed and arranged to send a messenger to Portsmouth. The messenger, George Allison, acting secretary of the Minority Movement, went to Portsmouth, but did not meet up with his fellow conspirators until the following day. During this period, however, he was being kept under observation by the police. The pamphlet was again discussed and Allison suggested the inclusion of a paragraph showing that the sailors fight against wage-cuts was similar to the agitation of the unemployed against restrictions in benefits. Suspicious of the sailors, Allison returned to Portsmouth on 2 October but was arrested and remanded. Bail was refused after the Chief Constable had objected.[131] Shepherd was arrested the following day in London and on 9 October both were remanded for a further week.The Chief Constable again opposed bail and it was refused despite the offer of substantial securities. They were charged under Section 1 of the 1797 Act and also with having conspired with Hugh Gerald Evelyn Hutchings to incite the sailors in His Majesty's Navy to mutiny, and on 10 October they were committed for trial. Bail was refused yet again, after the prosecutor had pointed out that one of the alleged conspirators was still at large.[132] Both men were found guilty and sentenced, Shepherd to 20 months imprisonment and Allison to three years penal servitude.[133]

Hutchings, whom his fellow conspirator Allison had never met, was not arrested until 24 October. A Superintendant intimated that the police would not oppose bail being granted and he was remanded on his own recognisance of £20 until 2 November, on which date he did not appear; the case was not called, the charge having been withdrawn.[134]

Curtis claims that Hutchings was a police spy, of whose existence the Portsmouth Police were unaware, but who was in the employ either of the Admiralty or the Special Branch.[135] The circumstantial evidence to support this is strong and it does seem likely that Hutchings thought he had caught two Communists, and two sailors into the bargain. He must have been very surprised to find that he rather than the sailors was involved in the alleged conspiracy.

Incitement to Disaffection and the Armed Forces 1931-4

While various security forces were apparently endeavouring to incite unsuspecting sailors and Communists to contravene the 1797 Act, MI5 did not miss the opportunity to campaign for new legislation. On 15 October, Colonel Holt-Wilson contacted the DPP, E.H. Tindal-Atkinson, to ask for assistance in drawing attention to the fact that the law 'has not kept step with recent developments in this very dangerous form of attack on the public welfare'.[136] He in turn sent a copy of this letter to the Home Office with a covering letter expressing the opinion that some further permanent legal powers were urgently needed 'even if only limited to matters in which His Majesty's Forces are concerned.'[137] After the Home Secretary, Sir Herbert Samuel, had seen it this letter was sent on to the Under Secretary of State for War, Sir Herbert Creedy, who informed the Home Office in April 1932 that the Secretary for War, Lord Hailsham (formerly Sir Douglas Hogg), had considered it (for five months) and had decided not to take any action in the matter by amending the Army Act. Nor was he in favour of promoting a special Bill.

This may appear surprising in view of Hailsham's past record in this area, but his reasons are particularly enlightening. The Army Act was subject to annual review, which meant that an amendment might be challenged or removed in subsequent years, and the offences would be created in an Act dealing with army discipline but tried in civil courts. As against legislation by a special Bill, Hailsham shrewdly observed that there were 'the disadvantages of a discussion at the present juncture and a possibility of the disclosure of the not inconsiderable powers already possessed by the Executive which might provoke comment and challenge'.[138]

In October 1932 a comprehensive report was made to the Home Office by one of the Security Services, dealing with 'the rising menace constituted by Communism to the Country and the inadequacy of the present law to deal with it'.[139] Most historians and other commentators on the Communist Party of Great Britain are of the opinion that, despite the inflated membership due to the unemployed, the CPGB had reached the nadir of its power and influence by this time.[140] The rhetoric of this report is an excellent example of exaggeration in the information presented to a Government by a 'security service'. This particular report was accompanied by a draft Public Security Bill, the substance of which was much wider than anything hitherto proposed. It extended to actions likely to cause disaffection in the civil service and *other* public services, or inducing, attempting to induce, or committing any act likely to induce any member of such services to 'fail in duty'. Although this phraseology is much more vague and capable of much wider interpretation than anything so far discussed, it is hardly surprising that the author of the report (not indicated) regarded this Bill as 'the minimum measure of legislation required'.[141] Nevertheless, it did not go further than Home Office discussions, even though MI5 informed the Army Council in May 1933 that by then it was even more essential to expedite the introduction of legislation.[142]

Throughout the 1920s the NUWM had organised the unemployed of Britain and, despite police violence and concerted Government opposition, had held several hunger marches to London from all over the Country.[143] The biggest of these marches reached London in October 1932. The Prime Minister adamantly refused to meet the marchers' leaders, but on 1 November a deputation was to go to the House of Commons with a million-signature petition against the means test and benefit cuts. There was widespread alarm in London, the press claiming that the unemployed had converged on London deliberately to cause trouble. A meeting in Trafalgar Square with an estimated attendance of 150,000 did not ease such fears and it was known that there would be a huge march to the Commons in support of the petition. Special Constables had been appointed in London, ostensibly to take over the the menial tasks of the police who might be occupied in other ways, but it became apparent that they were not simply an emergency ration. The Metropolitan Police were not happy about them either and felt that they might 'cause trouble rather than avoid it'.[144]

A Cabinet Committee had already been appointed to consider the whole question of the hunger marchers, how to get rid of them and how to stop them returning. In the meantime, the Special Branch were continuing their close watch on the NUWM offices and officials. On 1 November the offices were raided, but Wal Hannington, head of the movement, was not allowed to be present during the search and was given evasive answers to his requests to see a search warrant.[145] He was, in fact, taken to Bow Street Police Court and charged under Section 3 of the Police Act 1919, with attempting to cause disaffection among members of the Metropolitan Police. The evidence against him was a portion of a speech he had made at the meeting in Trafalgar Square. He had reminded the police that they were drawn from the working class and suggested that the special constables were ready to take over if the police went on strike against pay cuts. 'We ask the police to understand that what we are marching for is in their interest as well as the interests of the unemployed. We have marched to London for the abolition of the means test and the restriction in the pay of sailors, soldiers and policemen, as well as the unemployed. Let the working class in uniform and out of uniform stand together'.[146] He was remanded in custody for a week, bail being refused, and as he states in his book, it was not difficult to realise that the arrest had been made with the deliberate intention of removing him from the leadership, and disorganising the march. There were in fact a number of very violent confrontations with mounted and foot police and the million signature petition was confiscated as it arrived in several taxis at Charing Cross Station, never to be seen again.

Hannington was more than suspicious that the raid on the offices was designed to find a document which had been planted the night before, linking the NUWM with proposals for terrorist activities. He had immediately destroyed this, but amongst the 5cwt of documents seized by the police was a letter written by Sid Elias, another official, which he had sent from Moscow while there as a delegate at a Workers' Conference. In it, Elias had expressed his views on the steps that he thought might be taken to strengthen the activities of the hunger march. On the basis of this, Elias was charged with 'attempting to cause discontent and disaffection and ill-will between different class of His Majesty's subjects and to create public disturbances against the police'. He received the maximum sentence of two years imprisonment. When Hannington's own trial opened on 8 November at Bow Street, he cross-examined the police witnesses on the extent of disaffection in the Metropolitan Police Force, quoting extensively and effectively from several editions of *Police Review*, the organ of that Force. One officer stated that he was not aware of any dissatisfaction or disaffection in the force but went on to agree that he had read several articles which clearly stated the dissatisfaction of the police in relation to pay cuts. When Hannington pointed out the inconsistency of his statements, the magistrate, Sir Chartres Biron, intervened asking him not to continue that line of questioning.

Hannington submitted that he could not cause disaffection among the police if it was already there. As a matter of fact this was probably true, but the charge was not 'causing' but 'attempting to cause' and so far as that statutory offence is concerned the impossibility of causing, no matter how conclusive the evidence, is of no consequence. After a forceful speech from the dock in which he stated the reasons for the charge as he saw them, he was found guilty and sentenced to the maximum three months imprisonment.

Six weeks later the Cabinet Committee on the hunger marchers submitted an interim report to the Cabinet, dated 16 December.[147] The Attorney-General, Sir Thomas Inskip, had suggested that instead of resorting to new legislation, further trial should be given to the procedure under an Act of Edward III by which a Court of Summary Jurisdiction may order anyone to enter into a recognition and find sureties to keep the peace or to be of good behaviour. It was reasonable to suppose, he thought, that Magistrates would be willing to use these powers against leaders of the Hunger Marchers. By coincidence, Tom Mann, now national treasurer of the NUWM and Emrhys Llewellyn, secretary, were arrested under that Act on 17 December and, on refusing to be bound over on sureties of £200 and £100 respectively, were imprisoned for two months.

When the report was submitted to the Cabinet on 21 December, considerable importance was attached to its last recommendation, that the Committee should submit a further report on the existing powers relating to matters such as the importation of funds destined for seditious purposes and Communist propaganda in the services, which the Home Secretary, now Sir John Gilmour, had informed the Committee were inadequate.[148] Extensive search revealed no record of this Committee having met again to consider these matters or having reported on them.

It is evident that the National Government, or at least the Conservative members of it, were acutely aware of the power which their vast majority in the Commons bestowed upon them. They were now in a position to ensure the passage of legislation which no single party Government would even have introduced nor would be able to pass in the future. The feeling of urgency was made quite explicit by the Home Secretary, Sir John Gilmour, in suggesting to the Cabinet on 8 March 1933 reforms in the Metropolitan Police Force contained in a memorandum by the then Metropolitan Commissioner, Lord Trenchard.[149] The 1919 Act had outlawed the Police Union and substituted the Police Federation, the brainchild of Macready. By 1933 discontent was once more widespread in the force. Like other state employees and dependants, the police had suffered economy cuts – 5% in 1931 and a further 5% in Chamberlain's 1932 Budget. After the first cuts the Metropolitan Police Force had asked permission to hold a protest meeting at the Albert Hall. The Commissioner recommended that it should be permitted and the Home Secretary, Sir Herbert Samuel, informed the Cabinet on 25 September 1931 that too much importance need not be attached to it.[150] Such complacency, less than two weeks after the Invergordon sailors had demonstrated their dissatisfaction in such a dramatic fashion, and in any case, long before the memories of 1919 had faded, could only serve to increase the discontent which already existed. Wal Hannington argued a year later that dissatisfaction was widespread. Four months after that the Home Secretary agreed. 'Discipline in the force is bad; discontent is widespread; *esprit de corps* is almost entirely lacking; and the standard of efficiency . . . is far short of what it should be . . . Reform is urgently needed.' Lord Trenchard was convinced discontent was rife only because the representative machinery was fundamentally misconceived. It was 'being used as a rallying point for the discontented elements in the Police and as a legalised instrument for stirring up unrest and stimulating resistance to Government decisions'. His solution was as simple as his explanation – a short service scheme of ten years for constables, and direct entry for officers. The Federation could be dispensed with and the men would ventilate their grievances through their officers, 'the normal, natural channel'.[151]

Macready had had no doubt that some type of formal machinery was essential, and had introduced several other forms of a distinctly non-military character, including promotion from below right up to Chief Constable. Trenchard was now seeking to overturn all of this. It did not require great shrewdness to realise, as Gilmour did, that the suggested reforms would be strenuously resisted by the Metropolitan Branch Boards and by the Police Federation as a whole. Despite this, he was confident that they would be able to dispel any doubts that the recruitment of officers was 'a step in the direction of militarising the Police, or an anti-democratic scheme based on class-interest'.[152] The repercussions of the adoption of such a scheme would have been enormous. Britain's supposedly liberal democratic constitution was severely strained in the period between the wars. This could have been the first major breach in a systematic assault on this constitution, and the first step in the creation of an autocratic regime. The most alarming aspect of these proposals is not their apparent uniqueness, but that they were the logical development of other innovatory legislation of that period.

Probably the last case involving a charge under the 1797 Act was a prosecution in January 1933 of four South Wales miners, Stead, Paddock, Jeffries and Watley, who were members of the South Wales District Committee of the Communist Party. Stead was charged with conspiring with Paddock and Jeffries to endeavour to seduce soldiers from their duty or allegience. Watley was charged with conspiring with Jeffries to the same end. Jeffries and Paddock were charged with endeavouring to seduce soldiers from their duty and allegiance; and to complete the barrage of charges, all four were charged with conspiring together to that end.[153]

Although the alleged offences were committed in Monmouthshire and the committal proceedings were held in Newport, the four were committed for trial to the Old Bailey instead of their local assizes. The official reason was that it would be difficult to get a fair trial in Monmouthshire, but D.N. Pritt, KC, who defended the four, claimed that they were well known and popular in the area and may have been acquitted by a local jury.[154] By a strange coincidence the judge who was to preside in this fair trial turned out to be none other than Mr Justice Humphreys once again.

The star witness for the prosecution was a soldier in the Territorials named Lloyd. He was also secretary of the District Committee of the Communist Party and of the local branch of the NUWM, although he had resigned the latter post before the trial.[155] Although he was, in fact, a slaterer and plasterer and wore uniform only very occasionally, he appeared in the witness box in full uniform. On being questioned about this he indicated that he had been ordered to do so.[156] He agreed that he had written a letter in July 1932 to one of the accused saying: 'I am in a position to let you know any news concerning the Territorial Army you wish. I have free entry into three regimental clubs in Newport'. He was asked to distribute copies of the *Soldiers' Voice* among the troops and immediately took them to the Police. At the trial he agreed that he had received a few shillings from the police. A Detective-Inspector admitted that in all he had given Lloyd £6 to act as an informer.[157]

The Incitement to Disaffection Bill

At about this time an unofficial and informal conference of Ministers was held and arising from this a Bill, the Incitement to Sedition Bill, was drafted by Parliamentary Counsel.[158] After this Bill had been vetted by the Attorney-General, Sir Thomas Inskip, and his suggestions incorporated, it was sent, on 3 April by Gilmour to Hailsham at the War Office. Gilmour drafted a Memorandum in May 1933, and suggested that it should be a joint Memorandum to the Cabinet by himself, the

First Lord of the Admiralty, and the Secretaries for War and Air. In preparing it, the Home Secretary had obviously been strongly influenced by the arguments of previous proposers of such bills. He plagiarised large sections of previous reports and Memoranda as far back as the Public Order Bill of 1921.[159]

It was not until 9 October 1933 that the Memorandum and draft Bill were made known to the Cabinet. On that occasion the First Lord, Sir B. Eyres-Monsell, made a verbal report to the Cabinet to the effect that Communist agents known to the authorities had in their possession a pamphlet intended to be issued to the Fleet containing a 'gross incitement to mutiny'. After he had explained the inadequacy of the existing law to deal with this situation, the Home Secretary informed the Cabinet of the existence of the Bill and the Memorandum.[160] This is somewhat strange since the First Lord had been aware of both Bill and the Memorandum since May and had attended the Conference of Ministers from which the Bill derived. Macdonald, however, does not seem to have been aware of these discussions and it may well be that this was simply an opportune moment for his Conservative colleagues to inform him. When the Bill was introduced in the House the following year the Attorney-General attempted to convince MPs that it was a purely procedural measure. The joint Memorandum presented to the Cabinet on 18 March 1933 and dated 10 March, certainly gave the impression that the changes which the Bill would make were merely to facilitate the easier functioning of the law. In fact, it was stated at the end that the Bill, which had been drafted with the alternative of applying it to the Civil Service as well as the armed forces, should not so apply, because it would be creating new law, the implication being that the Bill did not create new law. This, as we shall see, was demonstrably untrue, and if this was designed to pull the wool over the eyes of the former Labour Party members in the Cabinet, it appears to have been singularly successful.

In approving the Bill, the Cabinet decided that the Law Officers should deal with it in the Commons and they were informed accordingly.[161] Having succeeded at last in gaining Cabinet approval for the introduction of such a measure, the War Office, the Air Ministry and MI5 became concerned about the possibility of disaffection amongst the civilian wardens employed at Military and Air Force stations. These, sworn in as Special Constables but appointed under Section 3 (1) of the Special Constables Act 1923, were not protected by Section 3 of the Police Act 1919, nor would they be by the proposed legislation.[162] No action was taken on this point, but at the end of February 1934 the Home Secretary proposed that the provisions of the draft Bill be extended to cover the civil police. He apparently felt that if 'the gap was closed' in the case of the defence services there would be 'an incentive to the instigators of sedition' to turn their attentions to the police unless the latter were also covered. In justification of his proposal, Gilmour explained that evidence had recently come to light suggesting that the police force 'contains at least a proportion of men who could not be relied on to withstand attempts to undermine their loyalty, and though the evidence that such attempts are being made is not so strong in the case of the Police as in the case of the defence services there can be no doubt that the risk of such attempts is a serious one'.[163]

It seems likely that Lord Trenchard had a hand in this proposal, but it was not warmly greeted by the Cabinet. It was criticised on two strangely contrasting grounds; that it potentially covered a very wide area of conduct, and that it would expose the Bill to a good deal of criticism and might even tend to jeopardise its passage.[164] No doubt it was the National Labour members who raised the first objection, but it is of no great consequence. The Prime Minister made an appeal to the Home Secretary not to press the matter unless he regarded it as absolutely essential and the latter agreed, but only on the understanding that he should have a right to re-open the question if necessary.[165]

The original bill had been drafted with alternative phrases in the first clause prescribing either attempts to cause sedition or disaffection amongst members of His Majesty's Armed Forces *or* endeavours to seduce such persons from their duty or allegiance. Before the Bill was printed on 16 March 1934, the second wording had been chosen. The long title of the Bill had read: 'A Bill to make better provision for prevention and punishment of the causing sedition or disaffection amongst His Majesty's Forces.' This was altered accordingly and no mention of sedition or disaffection remained in the Bill. The short title of 'Incitement to Sedition Bill' was now incongruous but the incongruity was not alleviated by the substitution of 'Incitement to Disaffection Bill' since Incitement and Disaffection are nowhere mentioned in the Act as passed.

The Bill was introduced into the Commons by the Attorney-General, the Solicitor General, the First Lord of the Admiralty, and representatives of the War Office and Air Ministry. The Secretaries for War and Air, Hailsham and Londonderry, were both in the House of Lords and the Home Secretary had claimed that his responsibility for the Bill ended when there was no longer any question of it covering the Civil Service or the Police.[166] In fact, full responsibility was placed squarely on the shoulders of the Law Officers, Sir Thomas Inskip and Sir Donald Somervell. One reason for this was that the Government hoped to pass the measure as an uncontroversial procedural Bill; without substantial evidence it would be difficult to convince the House that a considerable increase in executive power was now necessary, which had not been necessary in the preceding decade. The Government had no such evidence to present. The Attorney-General attempted to make the best use of available evidence but the statistics he offered showed, in fact, that the amount of communist propaganda distributed had decreased considerably in the period 1931-1932, as had the number of distribution places.[167]

Having saddled the Attorney-General and the Solicitor General with responsibility for this Bill, the Cabinet left them to face the opposition on their own. The Home Secretary had conveniently wiped his hands of it and MPs were not aware of the part which he had played in formulating the measure. Few of the members who voted for it were willing to make speeches in justification of it, while the Attorney-General himself must have been embarassed by the inadequacy of the only arguments he could produce. The Standing Committee sat on 14 days. The War Office was represented on four occasions only. The representatives of the Admiralty and the Air Ministry did not put in a single appearance. Twice the Government failed to obtain a quorum.

Most conspicuous for his absence during the debates on the Bill was the Prime Minister, who did not appear in the Chamber until the day on which the Bill passed its third reading. His presence that day was due to notice having been given of the intention of Major Milner (Labour, Leeds, SE) to read extracts from a letter written by Macdonald during the war to E.D. Morel after the latter had been imprisoned for pacifist activities. The Prime Minister's words had been quoted often during those debates but this apparently was too much for him. It was ironic that one correspondent to the *New Statesman* in July 1934, suddenly found that a project he had been planning was rendered illegal; he had collected all of Macdonald's war speeches with the intention of publishing extracts and distributing them to as many soldiers and sailors as possible.

The Prime Minister had his own version of the rationale of the Bill. In a letter to Ronald Kidd, secretary of the newly formed Council of Civil Liberties he claimed that 'it was designed to protect liberty and freedom of speech against movements of a kind similar to those that have appeared in country after country on the continent and which in some cases have led to the overthrow of democratic institutions'. Kidd in reply asked if he was aware that 'this Bill, capable of such repressive and tyrannical application in the hands of a reactionary government, is closely parallelled in modern continental legislation'.[168]

Protest against the Bill was far from being limited to the House of Commons. The newly formed Council for Civil Liberties, now the NCCL, organised and co-ordinated a massive campaign against the Bill which included two demonstrations in Trafalgar Square, a delegate conference and a joint deputation of representatives of the NCCL, the London Trades Council and the National Liberal Federation to the Attorney-General. On that occasion Inskip was obviously irritated by the precision of the questions which he was asked and to which he gave characteristically evasive answers.[169]

Public protest against the Bill was continued for seven months; thousands of groups, societies, clubs and trade union branches who appreciated the dangers of the Bill passed resolutions and held meetings and marches. People from all walks of life and of conflicting political persuasions joined together to defeat a common enemy. These included writers and intellectuals of the day such as H.G. Wells, J.B. Priestley, E.M. Forster, Kingsley Martin, Professor H.J. Laski, and W. Ivor Jennings. The list is endless, but when an eminent and notoriously conservative lawyer such as Sir William Holdsworth, KC, Vinerian Professor of English Law at Oxford, spoke out against the Bill, the Government was forced to listen respectfully. Even after amendment in Committee, Sir William referred to it as 'the most daring encroachment upon the liberty of the subject which the Executive Government has yet attempted at a time which is not a time of emergency'. His observations on the general significance of the introduction of the Bill are also worth recording here:

> 'The fact that such a bill could be introduced by a National Government, and still more the fact that such a Government should be surprised at the storm of indignation from persons of all parties which it has aroused, is a very disquieting feature of the mentality of the present day . . . because it shows that the statesmen of today are so much in the hands of bureaucrats, who run the departments of which these statesmen are the nominal heads, that they have contracted that limited vision which is the characteristic of the bureaucrat out to increase the efficiency of his department, and have for-

gotten the importance of those historic principles of Constitutional law, which from very early times, have safeguarded the liberties of the subject from the tyranny, bureaucratic or otherwise.'[170]

Several other lawyers spoke out against the Bill, including J.L. Brierley, Professor of International Law at Oxford; a manifesto against it was issued by seventeen barristers and solicitors; and the *Law Journal* protested editorially.[172] Almost all of the national newspapers and periodicals published articles of protest, although some were noticeably more muffled than others. The Army Council must have been alarmed to discover that several articles were published in the *Army, Navy and Air Force Gazette* for 1934 condemning the Bill outright as an unnecessary slur on the intelligence and loyalty of the services. Writing of seduction from duty which is not also seduction from allegiance or incitement to mutiny, Major Norman Parkes, barrister at law, stated, 'one wonders what type of dereliction of duty falling short of either of these is of such fundamental constitutional significance as to justify rendering incitement to it criminal. . . . It is the constitutionalist rather than the revolutionary who fears this Bill'.[175]

One of the popular cries in the House during the passage of the Bill was that the people of Britain would not have to wait for fascism to take away their liberties as the National Government was determined to remove them by legislation. In an unguarded moment, Walter Elliot, Minister of Agriculture and Fisheries, gave an interview to the Vienna *Neue Presse* in which he indiscreetly gave credence to this thesis. 'If one wants to introduce a new thing into this country one must do it as if it were an old thing. For that reason it seems to me to be courting failure to tell people that they have to dress themselves up in black shirts and throw their opponent downstairs in order to get the corporative (sic.) State. This new economic order has already been developed further in England than is generally recognised'.[174]

The Incitement to Disaffection Act 1934

Several contemporary authors claimed that the Attorney General had grossly mis-stated the law and misrepresented the changes which the Bill would make. This was undoubtedly true, but they were not prepared to blame the Attorney General and instead suggested that he had not been properly advised.[175] Sir Thomas would hear no criticism of his advisers and stated repeatedly that he accepted full responsibility for all that he had said. He was not a newcomer to the post of Law Officer; he had been Solicitor-General or Attorney-General from 1922 until 1934 with only two brief breaks during the Labour Administrations in 1923-4 and 1929-31. He more than anyone, therefore, must have been well acquainted with the history of this Bill and ought to have been well aware of its innovatory nature. He had also been consulted when the Bill was being drafted and some of the proposals were incorporated in it. If the misrepresentations were not deliberate attempts to mislead the House, the only conclusion is that Sir Thomas Inskip was a particularly bad lawyer. In 1939 he became Lord Chancellor as Lord Caldecote and from 1940 to 1946 he was Lord Chief Justice – the only man this century to have held both posts. Whether other Ministers ought to be excused for inaccurate statements as to the effects of legislation which they are promoting is an open question, but the constitutional responsibility of the Law Officers of the Crown when promoting legislation is to explain precisely the extent of legal innovations.

In the second reading debate the Attorney-General stated that it was 'perfectly plain that there is nothing novel or startling in clause one of this Bill, which merely sets out that which is already an offence but is an offence punishable only by indictment'.[176] This was urged repeatedly throughout the passage of the Bill, but it was, in fact perfectly plain that whereas the 1797 Act had made it an offence to endeavour to seduce soldiers from their 'duty *and* allegiance', this Bill said 'duty *or* allegiance'. Inskip resisted an amendment proposed by Dingle Foot to substitute 'and'.[177]

In drafting the first clause, the words 'maliciously and advisedly', which appeared in the 1797 Act, were omitted. This raised a howl of indignation in the House, since it meant that the Government proposed to remove the need for the prosecution to prove intention or to prove that the accused knew the person whom he endeavoured to seduce to be a member of the Forces. These words were then included, but such opposition probably took the Government completely by surprise. As shown earlier, the Home Secretary in 1919 refused to accept an amendment to clause three of the Police Bill, requiring the offence to be committed wilfully; since then no consideration had been given in any proposed legislation in this area to the requirements of intention or knowledge.

The original clause 2 (1) proscribed 'without lawful excuse' of documents which if disseminated among members of the Forces would constitute an offence under clause 1. Retention of 'without lawful excuse' would have meant that mere possession would have been an offence. MacColl and Wells argue that on the analogy of a prosecution under Section 7 (c) of the *Post Office (Protection) Act 1884,* which contained this phrase, the possessor of a document would have had to show that he did not know that it could be used to endeavour to seduce soldiers from their duty or allegiance: that is, he would have to show that he was ingnorant of its contents.

The Attorney-General was compelled to substitute for 'without lawful excuse' the words 'with intent to commit, or to aid, abet, counsel or procure the commission of an offence, under section one of this Act'. MacColl and Wells note that the original phrase 'without laeful excuse' derived from statutes which put the burden of justification on the possessors of property, like a forger's die, which is *per se* illegal. 'Any document, in other words, which might be used as an incitement to disaffection is regarded in Whitehall as criminal in its very nature . . . If you hold such documents, you hold them at your peril and you must expect no protection from the law in respect of them'. As the Attorney-General put it in *Elias v. Pasmore* (50 T.L.R., 196) discussing the documents seized at the N.U.W.M. offices in 1932, 'There could not be any property in any article which it was a crime to possess'. This was certainly the aim of the Army Council, but although the military authorities and the police appear to have acted as if it were also the law, that case demonstrated that they had exceeded their powers.

Clause 2 (2) of the Bill as introduced stated: 'If a person does or attempts to do or causes to be done or attempted, any act preparatory to the commission of an offence under section one of the Act, he shall be guilty of an offence under this Act'. The Attorney-General asserted that section 7 of the *Official Secrets Act 1920,* which the Lloyd-George Government had introduced, contained precisely the same provision in relation to 'an act preparatory'. That section however runs:

> 'Any person who . . . aids or abets *and* does an act preparatory to the commission of an offence under the principal Act or this Act, shall be guilty of . . .'.

This obviously makes it impossible to convict anyone of merely doing an 'act preparatory' unless he is also guilty of something in addition, viz. aiding and abetting. Clause 2 (2) of the 1934 Bill, on the other hand, would have made it quite possible to convict anyone of merely doing an 'act preparatory' without any other act at all. This, it was pointed out at the time, would make buying a train ticket an offence if the purpose of the journey was to distribute leaflets to soldiers. This sub-clause was eventually withdrawn.

Section 2 (2) of the Act gave the Police the wide powers of search, the absence of which had troubled the authorities. The joint memorandum to the Cabinet drafted by Sir John Gilmour stated that this was the most controversial but most essential part of the Bill.[178] It pointed out that the existing law contained no provisions for 'preliminary search in aid of evidence on which a charge could be based'. It did not point out that possession of the documents which they desired to seize had not hitherto been illegal.

At common law, with the single exception of cases where stolen goods are suspected of being on the premises, no magistrate has any power to grant a warrant for the general search of premises. This general principle has not been questioned since the case of *Entick v. Carrington* ((1765), 19 State Trials, 1030). Entick, the plaintiff, was arrested for sedition, under a warrant which also authorised the seizure of his books and papers. He brought an action against the King's messengers for trespass and Lord Camden condemned as illegal the warrant issued by Lord Halifax, a Secretary of State, and awarded Entick damages.

'If suspicion at large should be a ground for search', he said, 'whose house would be safe?' It was urged that the search warrant ought to be held legal, because it was useful to have means of providing evidence – 'I wish some cases had been shown', said the Lord Chief Justice, 'where the law forceth evidence out of the Owner's custody by process', – 'If a right of search for the sake of discovering evidence ought in any case to be allowed, this crime (seditious libel) above all others ought to be excepted, as wanting such a discovery less than any other'.[179]

Lord Camden clearly felt that such general search warrants should never be legal, because 'the secret cabinets and bureaux of every subject in this kingdom will be thrown open to the search and inspection of a messenger, whenever the Secretary of State shall think fit to charge, or even to suspect, a person to be the author, printer, or publisher of a seditious libel'.[180] The language was perhaps rather archaic in 1934, but the sentiments were just as true. 'Where is the written law that gives any magistrate such a power?' Camden had asked. Sir Thomas Inskip, having repeatedly argued that the warrant which he sought to legalise was not a General Warrant, stated in an unguarded moment that if any future Lord Chief Justice were to ask that question the passage of this Bill would enable the answer 'This is the authority for the magistrate' to be given.[181] Inskip seems to have thought that General Warrants were objectionable because the law made no provision for them. Lord Camden, however, had answered his own question: 'I can safely answer that there is none, and therefore it is too much for us without such authority to pronounce a practice legal which would be subversive of all the comforts of society'.[182]

Since Lord Camden's time there had been a number of statutory extensions of the power of search. MacColl and Wells note that these had fallen into two categories, extensions of the common law right of search for stolen property or authorisations of searches for articles the possession of which did *prima facie* imply a criminal object. 'Never had the legislature taken the risk of allowing the executive to search for articles in the undoubted possession of their rightful owner, a possession which may have a quite innocent explanation.'

The Attorney-General failed in his duty of giving impartial and accurate legal advice to the House by leading them to believe that the search warrant he wished to legalise was comparable to that under the *Obscene Publications Act 1857.* Whereas under that Act a Police Officer has to take a copy of the supposed obscene publication which has emanated from the premises he wishes to search, under the 1934 Act the police officer merely has to give an assurance that there is reasonable ground for suspecting that an offence has been committed.

During the First World War, DORA Regulations 51 and 51A contained extensive powers of search, some of which were revived in the defence regulations under the *Emergency Powers Act 1920.* The powers under DORA were, of course, available until August 1921 by which time the police had made considerable use of them. The lapse of

DORA does not seem to have interfered seriously with police habits. It is noted above that a vast quantity of material was seized in 1925 in the raids immediately before the arrest of the Communists. In cross-examination at that trial, Inspector Norwood of Scotland Yard said he had power to take what he liked, and he took whatever he thought necessary.[183] Detective-Sergeant Foster said, 'I thought it my duty to take all papers and examine them, returning those of a private nature'.[184] The protest made at that time by the Prime Minister of 1934, Ramsay Macdonald, is understandable. He said, 'Upon what ground did this trial rest? Honourable members must remember that it was preceded by a general search. It was none of your old-fashioned, stilted pieces of constitutional rectitude, when the search took place for a specific thing, and if the specific thing was not found nothing else was disturbed. No, that is an old habit, and an old prejudice of British constitutionalism, which the modern Tory Party has torn up like a scrap of paper'.[185]

At the same time the Government had attempted one further step towards complete freedom of search. Clause 30 (1) of the *Criminal Justice Bill 1925* introduced by Hicks, was so wide that it puts even section 2 (2) of the 1934 Act in the shade. Fierce opposition forced its withdrawal in the committee stage. Macdonald wrote in *Forward* that this clause was 'the most pernicious proposal ever made in modern times for the undermining of personal liberty'.

By 1929 the Home Office apparently considered such a measure unnecessary. 'We are informed that there is no specific statutory sanction for this practice, although the view was expressed by the representatives of the Home Office that it had by long use become part of the law'.[186]

Five years later precisely the same argument was put forward in *Elias v. Pasmore,* (50 T.L.R., 196) which arose out of the seizure of documents in 1932 from the NUWM offices. Of the five hundred-weight of material seized, most was returned within a week, but some was retained by the police and used for the purpose of prosecuting Elias. These documents were not returned after the trial was over, and Elias brought an action for the return of the documents and damages for trespass *ab initio,* on the basis that an entry into premises which is initially lawful (in this case to arrest Hannington) becomes unlawful if illegalities are committed after entry. Mr. Justice Horridge decided against the plaintiffs and held that the entry was lawful to begin with and had not been made unlawful by anything which followed. He did, however, give judgment for the plaintiffs against all the defendants, including the Commissioner, Lord Trenchard, for the detention of the documents. D.N. Pritt, KC, who with Sir Stafford Cripps was counsel for the plaintiffs, argued later this 'substantial victory for civil liberty was more apparent than real', since it established the right of the police in law to seize documents which would be evidence against someone rather than the person whom they had gone to the premises to arrest.[187] The Attorney General in this case attempted to justify the right of search and seizure which the police claimed by asserting that they could not perform their dutues 'unless the right continued, which has been exercised as long as memory extends . . . namely, the right to take, on the arrest of a person, articles wherever they found them'.

The objections to the search clause in the Bill were not only against the principle but against the way in which the warrant was to be granted. It was originally to be available to any Constable who satisfied any Magistrate that he had reasonable ground for suspicion. Admittedly, the constable was required to give this information on oath but, despite the predictable platitudes about the virtues of members of the constabulary which came from the Bill's supporters, this was not generally accepted as a sufficient safeguard against abuse of power. Although the Attorney-General would not consider the possibility that the British Police could dabble in corruption or succumb to the temptation of abusing power, the requirement in the clause was amended to read 'an officer of rank not lower than that of Inspector'. It was widely understood that magistrates, lay JPs, were unlikely to be politically impartial and thus the requirement for issue of the warrant was altered, first to two magistrates, and subsequently to a Judge of the High Court.

Several other amendments were proposed which would have provided safeguards, including the requirement of independent witnesses at the search. The Solicitor-General, however, thought that 'our dislike of unnecessary prying into other people's affairs would make this duty one which would be very repugnant and is very much out of accord with our legal system'. He did not feel the same about General Searches and the only amendment which the Attorney-General was willing to accept was the present section 2 (2) (b) requiring the officer conducting the search to notify the owner if not present and provide a list of articles seized.

The only truly procedural innovation contained in the Act was to allow offences to be tried summarily. The Authorities had been hoping to achieve this since the early 1920s because they wished to deal with offenders more quickly and less ostentatiously then was possible on indictment under the 1797 Act. They had also wished to dispense with jury trial because it was always a potential threat to conviction; this was achieved in this Bill simply by making the maximum penalty on summary conviction lower than four months, which would allow the accused the option of trial by jury. Such was the outcry of the opposition at the thought of alleged offenders being tried by benches of biased magistrates, that the Attorney-General was forced to increase the penalty by one month to allow the option of jury trial. It should be noted that the maximum penalty on summary conviction in other legislation discussed above was or still is three months.

The Attorney-General's refusal to substitute 'and' for 'or' in Section 1 made the Act much wider than the 1797 Act by covering matters which had nothing to do with allegiance and might be trifling. That the innovatory character of this was not as great as the statutes themselves suggest is due to the fact that some of the prosecutions discussed above necessitated very liberal interpretation of the 1797 Act in order to secure convictions. 'Duty' and 'Allegiance' are entirely distinct concepts but they were not always treated as such by the courts. Yet the 1797 Act, could never have been stretched to cover all that the 1934 Act potentially covers. Pacifist literature, which does not seek to seduce from allegiance or incite to mutiny but does suggest disobedience by individual soldiers to specific orders would come within the provision of the 1934 Act.

The amendment of the clause relating to possession of documents limited the application of sub-section 2 (1) by placing on the prosecution the onus of proving that the accused intended to commit, assist or procure the commission of an offence under section 1. It is still very wide, however, and is not limited in any way by the type of document or its ostensible purpose. Inskip refused to accept an amendment limiting it to documents specially drafted for distribution to the troops. The sub-section absolves the prosecution from the necessity of proving any acts by the accused other than actual possession and in effect makes mere intention punishable. Since in most cases intention would have to be inferred from the acts of the accused, the mere possession of documents may give rise to the presumption of an intention and in order to rebut that presumption the possessor would have to *prove* that he did not intend to commit or to aid, abet, counsel or procure the commission of an offence under Section one. The limitation by the amendment is then illusory in most cases.

In a prosecution under Section 2 (1) of the Act the Crown must prove that the distribution of the documents amongst members of the forces would constitute an offence under Section 1, that the accused had such documents in his possession or under his control and the accused intended to distribute or to assist in or procure the distribution of such documents.

It is important to appreciate the type of literature which could conceivably come within the scope of this Act. Above, it was suggested that any literature which might influence a member of the forces to consider his job in any perspective other than simple obedience of his superiors was considered 'insidious'. It would not be an exaggeration to represent this as the scope of sections 1 and 2 (1) of the 1934 Act. Pacifist literature would certainly be covered, and in that category must be included the Bible, at least with pacifist passages underlined; pacifists were prosecuted during the First World War for distributing copies of the Bible with the Sermon on the Mount underlined. Obviously a great deal of socialist, communist and anarchist literature would be included, whether academic works, novels or poems. It is interesting to note that one relevant DORA regulation included stage productions and films and the first attempt to perpetuate the regulations in the Army Act of 1919 also included these before it was introduced in the House. As the wording of the Obscene Publications Act has been held to cover films there is no reason to suppose that films and stage productions could not be considered endeavours to seduce members of the forces from their duty or allegiance. Since in law a person is held to intend the natural and probable consequences of his actions, the performing or showing of an anti-military play or film in a town where a large number of soldiers were stationed could he held to contravene the Act, just as indiscriminate leafleting or distribution of the Bible in such circumstances could so be held. It has already been shown that the 1797 Act extended to what was considered to be legitimate and proper political propaganda. Admittedly, 'endeavouring to seduce from duty' is not capable of such wide interpretation as 'inciting to disaffection' would have been, but the borderline between criminal endeavours to seduce from duty to allegiance and legitimate political propaganda is never likely to be absolutely clear.

No prosecution under the Act takes place without the consent of the DPP and where a prosecution is being carried on by the DPP, a court of summary jurisdiction is not permitted to deal with the case summarily without the consent of the DPP. The Government would not accept an amendment requiring the Attorney-General's consent instead of the DPP's. It was argued that, since the offence is one against the State, the chief Legal Officer of the State ought to be the one to authorise the proceeding. The DPP, in any case, acts on the instructions of the Attorney-General and it is the latter who is responsible to the House. this was probably the reason why it was not desirable to have the Attorney-General openly responsible for the prosecutions under the Act. The Solicitor-General avoided these pointes by explaining that 'the Government had chosen the great officer of the State whose sole business is to judge in these cases whether on the evidence he thinks it sufficiently clear that a breach of the law as laid down by this House has been committed, and to make up his mind on that question'. Another point had been scored in favour of the myth of Executive exclusion from the institution of legal proceedings.

Whenever the DPP is carrying on a prosecution under the Act, he may insist upon the committal of the accused to trial by the High Court. This means, in effect, an announcement by the DPP to the Court, which will try the case that he regards the particular offence as serious. As the *New Statesman* said in 1934 'There could hardly be a worse way of beginning what is by its very nature a political trial.'[188]

The Operation of the Act 1934-73

After fifteen years of almost continuous effort on the part of the Army Council, the Security Services and various Ministers, they acquired the powers deemed necessary to deal with the Communist menace. Had propaganda amongst the forces continued at a level sufficient to concern the authorities, we might have expected immediate prosecutions. The reason why there were no prosecutions for three years must be left to speculation, but there are three equally plausible possibilities: that the Act had an immediate deterrent effect; that the opposition during the passage had shown the Government that prosecutions would be inexpedient; that such communist propaganda had, in fact, faded out before the passage of the Act.[189]

Whatever the reason, the first prosecution did not take place until March 1937. The impropriety of it is quite obvious from the facts.[190] An eighteen year old economics student from Leeds, Ronald Phillips, had a conversation with one Corporal Crabtree of the RAF in a railway station cafe and formed the opinion that Crabtree was disillusioned with the air force. In this he was clearly led on by the latter, who stated that he was 'going Bolshevik'. At one point the discussion centred on the possibility of stealing a plane and flying to Spain to help the Republicans, and Phillips later wrote to Crabtree suggesting that if he really felt 'revolutionary' he could either fly to Madrid 'on the sly' or stay in England and convert the whole squadron. He claimed that Soviet Russia was 'a marvellous place and is keeping up a terrific army and RAF (sic.) and the letter ended, 'I hope you will one day lead the men of Britain to victory. This is not twaddle'.

At the subsequent trial under Section 1 of the Act, Phillips told the Court that he was too young to be a member of the CPGB and that in any case would probably not be accepted as he held 'ultra-revolutionary' views not acceptable to orthodox Communists. It was not suggested that he had ever attempted to communicate with any other member of the forces, but Mr. Justice Singleton stated, 'You have pleaded guilty to an offence which strikes at the very safety of the Realm'. One might imagine a hint of sarcasm in these words had he not then sentenced Phillips to twelve months imprisonment.

The severity of this sentence aroused strong protest throughout the country and the Home Secretary subsequently reduced it to a few months. It must be remembered that the DPP's consent was necessary for this prosecution to take place, which presumably means that at least the Attorney-General, Sir Donald Somervell, had also consented.

On the outbreak of War in 1939 the *Emergency Powers (Defence) Act* was passed to provide the Executive with the powers which it desired, by the issuing of Regulations.[191] Regulation 39A superceded the 1934 Act for the duration of the emergency, and was, in fact, considerably wider in its application than the Act. It extended to 'persons engaged in any public authority in the performance of functions in connection with the defence of the realm' and added two new provisions. As from 9 May 1940 it became an offence, first, to 'endeavour to incite persons who have become or may become liable under the *National*

Service (Armed Forces) Act 1939 to be called up for service to evade any duties or liabilities which they are or may become liable to perform or discharge', under that Act and, second, to 'endeavour to incite persons to abstain from enrolling voluntarily in His Majesty's Forces or in any civil defence organisation or endeavour to prejudice the training, discipline or administration of those Forces or of any such organisation'. As *Civil Liberty*, the organ of the NCCL, pointed out in June 1940, it was an offence, punishable with two years' imprisonment, to incite persons to avoid conscription even though the steps advised to be taken would in themselves be perfectly legal and constitutional: 'The line between "inciting" and merely giving information may be very shadowy in actual practice'.

It also made it an offence to incite persons to refrain from becoming, for instance, ARP wardens, or to suggest to such persons that their conditions of service were not all that they might be. As Government control extended to more and more undertakings the categories of persons covered by these provisions became more and more extensive and the NCCL, carrying on a relentless campaign against these Regulations, warned that unless their withdrawal could be secured, the traditional British liberty of freedom of speech would be swept away.[192] The Regulations effectively ruled out pacifist propaganda during the war, and the activities of the Peace Pledge Union and other organisations were closely watched by the Special Branch.

The PPU was prosecuted in June 1940, on account of a poster which had been issued two years before. It read, 'War will cease when men refuse to fight: what are you going to do about it?' Four representatives of the PPU undertook to sign a resolution passed by the Council of the Union withdrawing the poster and were bound over for twelve months. The Attorney-General, Sir Donald Somervell, submitted in court that a poster publicly displayed is clearly intended to be read by everyone 'and in these days would be read by members of the Forces . . . the only persons whose refusal to fight would make any effect on war or indeed on anything else are those who may be ordered to fight'. The Magistrate was in no doubt that an offence had been committed: 'However cleverly the defendants might subsequently prove to themselves that they had no intention of affecting His Majesty's forces, if they had reflected for a moment they must have known that such a poster might possibly cause disaffection in the ranks of the fighting forces'.[193] The wording of Section 1 of the 1934 Act is certainly wide enough for this prosecution to be repeated under it in peacetime.

Other prosecutions under Regulation 39A did take place; in one, a conscientious objecter had made a speech in which he declared he would refuse to fight and advised others to do so, adding that soldiers were nothing but murderers;[194] in another, the accused told a soldier he had seen troops coming back from Dunkirk, many of them young and crying. 'You are fools to fight,' he added, 'I would welcome the downfall of the British Empire, because that would free the workers. I am a communist.'[195] There was one prosecution in 1944 of a former BUF member who had distributed pamphlets of speeches of Hitler, Goering and Goebbels. He had stated that the German forçes alone stood between Europe and Bolshevism and was found to possess lists of ships and cruisers sunk by the enemy.[196] A fourth case was reported in *Peace News*,[197] but the prosecution refused to read out the contents of a leaflet which had been thrown through a train window onto the lap of a passenger in uniform, as it would have given publicity to its 'mischievous views'.

The only prosecution under this Regulation which has achieved any degree of notoriety was that of the Freedom Press in 1945, shortly before the Regulation expired. On 12 December 1944, a squad of Special Branch Officers raided the premises of the Freedom Press and proceeded to remove everything, including the typewriter, account books and other material without which it was impossible to carry on the business. At the same time raids were made on the houses of five people connected with the Freedom Press and searches were made in the kits of soldiers and sailors stationed in Lancaster, Leamington, Derby and the Orkneys. These latter searches had been undertaken at the request of 'higher authority' with specific instructions to remove copies of *War Commentary* and other Freedom Press publications. Other literature, including *The Scots Socialist, The Bulletin, The New Statesman* and *The News Leader* were also taken.

About one hundred members of the Forces were subscribers to *War Commentary* which was published by the four anarchists who made up the Freedom Press, Dr. John Hewetson, Vernon Richards, Marie Louise Berneri and Philip Sansom. The evidence principally relied upon consisted of certain issues of *War Commentary* and other publications of the Freedom Press containing articles dealing partly with historical events, such as revolts which occurred at the end of the first World War and partly with resistance movements in Europe at the time of publication. They advocated the formation of Workers' Councils and advocated that soldiers should hold on to their rifles on returning home. The prosecution was unable to call any witnesses prepared to state that the articles had caused disaffection and the defence counsel strenuously denied any attempt to cause disaffection. Marie Louise Berneri was discharged on a technicality and the other three were sentenced to nine months imprisonment each.[198]

Philip Sansom has recently set out his own opinion of why this particular prosecution was instituted against what was a very small organisation not really capable of causing widespread disaffection in the Forces.[199] On entering prison they found that the cells were already full of soldiers who had deserted in Europe rather than continue fighting after the enemy had to all intents and purposes been defeated: disaffection was already widespread in the Forces. No doubt also, the authorities remembered the trouble after the first World War and the appeal which had then to be made for weapons to be returned.

After the Defence Regulations had expired, Incitement to Disaffection sank into obscurity. There was no prosecution for such an offence for almost thirty years, but there was one temporary extension of the provisions in 1951, presumably a preparation for involvement in Korea. Section 6 of the *Reserve and Auxiliary Forces (Training) Act* (the 'Z Bill' or 'Gag Bill') re-enacted the whole of the 1934 Act with only two alterations. Sub-section 1 read:

> "if any person maliciously and advisedly incites persons called up or liable to be called up under this part of this Act to failure in the performance or to evasion, of duties or liabilities under this part of this Act which they are, or may become, liable to perform or discharge, he shall be guilty of an offence under this section."

This, it was calculated, extended the provisions of the 1934 Act to cover 4,500,000 civilians. Despite the memory of the 1934 Bill the Government had originally omitted the words, 'maliciously and advisedly', even though the Prime Minister, Mr. Attlee, had been a vice president of the NCCL in 1934 and had spoken strongly against the Incitement to Disaffection Bill in the Commons.

The NCCL called a conference to protest against the Bill and 200 representatives of Trade Union branches, trades councils, peace committees, Co-op guilds and other democratic organisations attended. The Press, however, had largely forgotten its traditional self-proclaimed role as the watchdog of liberty and even protests in the House did not shake all of them out of their complacency. The *Daily Worker* ran the only editorial on the subject (KILL THIS BILL!) and was the only paper to publish a statement by the NCCL recalling the public outcry over the 1934 Act.[200]

The one other innovation in this Act was that the Attorney-General was made directly responsible for prosecutions. This may be one reason why there were, so far as has been ascertained, no prosecutions under Section 6.

The first prosecution under the original 1934 Act after the Phillips case did not take place until 1972. In May of that year an anarchist, Michael Tobin, was given the maximum penalty of two years imprisonment at Maidstone following a conviction under section 2(1). The pamphlets which formed the basis of the charge were called 'A Letter from a Ballymurphy Mother' and 'A letter from a soldier of the IRA to soldiers of the Royal Green Jackets'. The latter contained explicit appeals to soldiers to desert and offered a soldier £50 to go over to the IRA, £25 for delivering up an officer, and £80 for delivering up arms. Tobin, in conducting his defence, openly declared that 'a useful job would have been done if their distribution led to a questioning of the real aims and actions of the British Government in Northern Ireland'.[201]

In January 1972, however, Joseph Durkin, who admitted drafting these pamphlets and, it seems, distributing them by post, was acquitted at Liverpool Crown Court. He told the court that the letters were intended to reach officers of the Royal Green Jackets and not other ranks. He said he was not trying to cause disruption or unrest, but to gain publicity about English Concentration Camps. If the letters had fallen into the hands of soldiers, he added, they would say it was ridiculous. He continued, 'It would never enter the head of any soldier to leave his fellow men. They would just laugh at it'.[202]

It seems that only the two distinct lines of defence – one adamantly aloof and the other decidedly obsequious – distinguish the conviction from the acquittal. The evidence against Durkin was greater than against Tobin. The latter was refused leave to appeal against conviction, was adopted by a Swiss section of Amnesty International as a political prisoner and on serving his sentence complained to the European Commission on Human Rights that the British Government had prevented him from exercising his rights to freedom of expression. By that time the British Government was already determining the limitation of other people's right to freedom of expression.

THE OPERATION OF THE ACT SINCE 1973

In 1973 the British Withdrawal from Northern Ireland Campaign was formed by a group of pacifists, the aims, as the name suggests, being the withdrawal of British military presence in Northern Ireland and the end of the political union between Britain and Northern Ireland. The primary method used by the supporters of the campaign was the distribution of leaflets among soldiers to inform them of ways of leaving the army. The original BWNIC leaflet entitled 'Some Information for British Soldiers' contained fairly comprehensive factual information on various legal and illegal methods of leaving the army, including going absent without leave to Sweden, Eire, Britain or other countries, conscientious objection, and discharge on other grounds. It began and ended with more overtly political statements:

> 'We are aware that there are British soldiers who are leaving the army, or who want to, because of British policy in N. Ireland. We are glad about this and hope many more will do so . . . '
>
> 'A soldier who publicly stated that he refused to serve in N. Ireland, whatever the consequences, would be setting an example . . . Better still if a group of soldiers made this announcement simultaneously it would make a great impact on public opinion . . . Such an action could lead to Court Martial and imprisonment. But soldiers who believe, as we do, that it is wrong for British troops to be in N. Ireland are asked to consider whether it is better to be killed for a cause you do not believe in or to be imprisoned for refusing to take part in the conflict'.
>
> '. . . We who are distributing this fact sheet to you hope that, by one means or another, you will avoid taking part in the killing in N. Ireland'.[203]

During 1973 names and addresses of several leafletters were taken and they were warned to stop. Then in August 1973, Pat Arrowsmith was arrested in Colchester for insulting behaviour (distributing the leaflet) under the *Public Order Act 1936,* and told that the matter would be reported to the DPP for his consent to a prosecution under the 1934 Act. The Director decided not to give his consent and Arrowsmith was acquitted of the offence of insulting behaviour. Believing that the Director's decision implied that distribution of the leaflet was not actionable under the 1934 Act, BWNIC supporters continued to distribute copies.

However, only a week after the acquittal, Arrowsmith was again arrested, having been found with three other people distributing the leaflet in the married quarters of the School of Infantry, Warminster.

All four were taken into custody but only Arrowsmith, having persisted in distributing the leaflet after the civilian police arrived, was charged; this time for behaviour likely to cause a breach of the peace. After several months she was informed that she was also to be charged on two counts under Sections 1 and 2 of the 1934 Act.

The trial was held at the Old Bailey and lasted for a week from 13 to 20 May 1974.[204] None of the military witnesses who had received a copy of the leaflet was able to assert that he had in any way been influenced by it, but, of course, that was not necessary under the Act, which makes the endeavour the substantive offence. In fact, Judge Abdela disapproved of defence counsel's cross-examination on this point and after it became clear that no evidence about the political situation in Ireland or the question of whether distribution of the leaflet was increasing or decreasing disaffection could be led, defence counsel withdrew from the case. The new counsel contended, *inter alia,* that the leaflet was essentially informative and that there was no intention of seducing soldiers from their duty or allegiance. Arrowsmith agreed in cross-examination, however, that even if she had been convicted at Colchester, she would still have continued to leaflet soldiers because it was her duty to draw their attention to the Geneva Convention on methods of warfare.

The jury was instructed by Judge Abdela not to speculate about the conflicting decisions of the DPP. Clearly the Director is not a judicial authority and a decision by him not to prosecute must be taken to mean no more than that. He might have been expected, nevertheless, to give a warning that the distribution of the leaflet probably constituted an offence or that continued distribution might result in prosecution. He was later subjected to judicial criticism for not taking action in the first place.

The most extraordinary aspect of this production emerged in the evidence of Wendy Butlin, who was one of the three others taken into custody at Warminster. On being asked to desist from distributing leaflets, she had done so. The implication was that it was Arrowsmith's refusal to desist which had led to the prosecution rather than the action she was tried for. This aspect of the case was emphasised by the judge in his summing up. The DPP had obviously hoped to contain the leafletting in this way.

Crown counsel stressed the use of phrases such as 'we hope' and 'we are glad' – were not these encouragements rather than mere information? The leaflet opened by quoting the words of two ex-soldiers who had served in Northern Ireland and believed British military involvement there was wrong. Counsel argued that this was encouragement by example – very like the army information booklet *Northern Ireland: What is it like for Soldiers* which quotes soldiers who are already there and 'lap it up', feel it has 'been worth while coming' and simply 'enjoy it'.

Evidence of character on Arrowsmith's behalf was given by Lords Soper and Brockway, Hugh Jenkins MP, and Bernadette McAliskey. McAliskey described a meeting at which, she said, Arrowsmith had advised representatives of both the Official and Provisional IRA to desist from violence, which could only exacerbate the political situation, and to adopt non-violent means of struggle.[205] Although Judge Abdela had freely acknowledged the distinction between the present case and the IRA ones in 1972 (which Crown counsel was not aware of), referring to Bernadette McAliskey's evidence in his summing up, he noted that 'apparently with some ease, contact had been made with the IRA. This gives some indication of the politics that sits like an umbrella over this case'. This was a highly misleading, and improper innuendo and in the light of it, it is not surprising that the jury returned a unanimous guilty verdict. Pat Arrowsmith was sentenced to eighteen months imprisonment.

On 4 December 1974 the Court of Appeal, dismissing Arrowsmith's appeal against conviction, held *inter alia,* that it was a defence to a charge under the 1934 Act that the accused had acted under a mistake of fact but since Ms. Arrowsmith knew the contents of the leaflet and had intended to distribute it, she had made no mistake about the facts constituting the offence charged. The mistaken belief that she would not be prosecuted was not a mistake about the facts constituting the offence. The Appeal against sentence was allowed, however, since she had grounds for thinking it was unfair and it was reduced to nine months allowing her immediate release, 'so that justice was not only done but appeared to be done'.[206]

Some of the comments of Lord Justice Lawton during the hearing of the appeal are worthy of serious consideration. He described the argument that the leaflet was intended simply to give information to soldiers who were already disaffected as 'an insult to the intelligence of the jury'. He could not understand why the DPP had decided not to prosecute in the first instance since the leaflet was 'the clearest incitement to mutiny and desertion'. Having asserted that the court was not in any way concerned with the political background against which the leaflet was distributed, he explained that the real concern was 'the likely effects on young soldiers aged eighteen, nineteen, or twenty, some of whom may be immature emotionally and of limited political understanding'.

The question of the political maturity of young servicemen is a very relevant one, and not a new one. In 1950, the Labour MP, Raymond Blackburn, raised the subject in connection with an eighteen-year-old soldier serving in Korea. The matter was then taken up by all political parties, and the Government ordered that no soldier under nineteen should go to Korea.[207] At the very least it is doubtful whether it is fair to load a teenage soldier with the heavy political responsibility of orderly action in the streets of Northern Ireland. The problem is a very serious one, and was merely shelved by Lord Justice Lawton's revealing remarks.

After the Arrowsmith conviction, the BWNIC leaflet was revised, updated and reprinted under the title 'Some Information for Discontented Soldiers'. (See Appendix.) The factual information it contains is much more comprehensive than its predecessor and the beginning and end were re-written to stress the fact that it was addressed to 'discontented soldiers', that is, that it was not an endeavour to seduce but an aid to soldiers who had already decided what they wanted to do.

The reaction to Pat Arrowsmith's sentence was increased activity and the leafletting of barracks all over the country. At several places the leafletters had their names taken and in Aldershot three people were arrested for infringing a military bye-law by giving out leaflets on military land. On 6 July 1974 seven BWNIC supporters were arrested by the police at an army camp near Oswestry. Copies of the leaflet, which six of them had been distributing, were seized and forwarded with their names and addresses to the DPP. Apart from this, the leafletting campaign continued unhindered until 10 September when the homes of several campaign supporters were raided. Early in October six people were charged under section 2(1) of the 1934 Act.[208] By the beginning of November another six had been charged under section 2(1) and a further two people had been charged with conspiring between January 1973 and September 1974 to commit offences under the 1934 Act. This last charge was extended to cover all the accused, now numbering fourteen: Albert Beale, Wendy Butlin, Juliet Hornsby, John Hyatt, Chris Roper, Gwyn Williams, Phil Cadbury, Frank Keeley, Ronnie Lee, Paul Seed, Rick Walker, Mike Wescott, Bill Hetherington and Bob Thomas.

These fourteen were charged with conspiracy to contravene the 1934 Act. As has been shown, this type of prosecution is not uncommon in cases in this area of law. Almost all of the prosecutions discussed above have involved charges of conspiracy. There is no doubt in general that the use of conspiracy charges make it easier for the prosecution to obtain a conviction, and that where a conviction is proved against one or more of the alleged conspirators the others can be corralled with them. In a recent NCCL pamphlet on the subject, Geoff Robertson says

> 'There are three fundamental precepts of criminal law in a democratic society; its meaning and scope should be reasonably clear, it should express the will of the elected representatives of the people, and its procedure should conform to accepted standards of fairness. The conspiracy charge traduces each of these precepts'.

And further:

> 'The danger posed to society by the existence of a dragnet law which lacks certainty, democratic origins and procedural fairness, is potentially very grave. It authorises trial and imprisonment of critics of conventional authority and value systems, in the same way as "public safety" legislation bolsters executive tyranny in communist and fascist countries'.[209]

In as much as it was a major trial, and was well publicised in the national media, the trial of the 'BWNIC 14' was a major test both of the Incitement to Disaffection Act and of the conspiracy laws. The accused were committed for trial from Lambeth Magistrates Court in March 1975, and the trial itself took place at the Old Bailey from 29 September until 10 December 1975. In addition to the range of Incitement to Disaffection charges, two of the defendants, Gwynneth Williams and John Hyatt, were accused under the *Army Act 1955* of giving help to two different soldiers who were absent without leave.

The trial was made the centrepiece of an extremely political defence campaign, the BWNIC Defence Group, which occupied itself through 1975 with attempting to publicise the prosecutions, and in so doing helped to spawn a series of further charges against campaigners in Manchester, Preston and Arbroath (see below). Against this insistent background, it was therefore inevitable that the Old Bailey trial would contain many conflicts about the political character of the charges, and hence about the admissibility of certain types of evidence – conflicts which had already been raised during the Arrowsmith hearings.

Early in the trial, several of the defendants drew attention to the conflict by refusing to plead, on the grounds that the charges themselves contravened human rights. Michael Westcott, an eighteen year-old defendant from Birmingham, stated: 'I plead for peace in a world of war, love in a world of hate, free speech for all, and an end to politically motivated trials in this country'. To this, the judge, Neil McKinnon QC, retorted that if Westcott did not take care, a medical report on him would have to be ordered. This exchange, provoking as it did a condemnatory comment in the press by the Chairman of Amnesty International, set the political tone in which a variety of skirmishes took place between campaigners and the trial judge.[210]

In September 1975, a number of left-wing and pacifist papers had deliberately taken the step of publishing in full the text of the leaflet, 'Some Information for Discontented Soldiers'.[211] On 8 October, two demonstrators were arrested outside the Old Bailey for handing out leaflets in the street saying 'Defend the 14. Defend free speech. Drop the charges'. The two demonstrators, who were part of a leafletting campaign which continued throughout the course of the trial appeared in the dock with a banner saying 'Drop the charges'. The trial judge warned that these leaflets 'amount to contempt', rebuked them for suggesting that the defendants could be sentenced to life imprisonment for conspiracy, but released them. The NCCL condemned this action as an attempt to harass the exercise of freedom of speech.[212]

On 1 November, the NCCL showed a film, 'So You Think It's A Free Country?', on BBC-2's *Open Door* series. This film included newsreel about the trial's opening, showed an illegible photocopy of the contentious leaflet, attacked the Incitement to Disaffection Act as a bar on freedom of speech and information, and discussed a soldier's problems in trying to get discharged from the Army. As in the leafletting incidents, Judge McKinnon stated in court that there was material in the film, 'which may amount to contempt of court'. However, because the possible contempt would not have been a contempt in the face of the court, the judge had to refer the subject to the DPP to decide. After a three-day hiatus, during which the trial hardly advanced at all, the DPP decided not to prosecute the NCCL and the BBC since there was no contempt in the film, but even then the Clerk of the Court warned that the showing of the film might constitute grounds for the judge dismissing the jury and ordering a retrial.[213]

These important incidents, which received general publicity and revealed some of the problems inherent in a political trial, were nevertheless secondary to the remorseless 51-day hearing of the charges. The prosecution argued that 'Some Information for Discontented Soldiers' would probably not 'attract the dedicated patriot but it is designed to attract the waverer', whilst the substantive defence countered that the leaflet was purely informative about soldiers' ways of leaving the army. Most of the charges referred to the handing out of the leaflets. One defendant, Robert Thomas, was unlucky enough to put a copy through the letterbox of a retired Major-General in Devizes, who promptly took him to the police station.[214]

The defence case rested on four central arguments. The first was that the contentious leaflets were not seductive documents. Second, that the British Withdrawal from Northern Ireland Campaign had never intended to seduce soldiers, and evidence was produced in court from internal campaign documents which showed that there was a policy of not giving persuasive or didactic material to soldiers. Third, that no soldier was produced in court to say that any of the defendants had attempted to seduce him from duty or allegiance, or that any of the leaflets had had that effect. Fourth, and most important, was the emphasis in the defence upon the personal commitment and principle of the defendants. As Tony Gifford, one of the defence counsel, put it to the jury: 'you cannot really convict them without convicting a whole tradition in society of being fraudulent'. Other defence counsel also attempted to place the trial in the context of the history of freedom of speech trials in this country dating from the 18th century.[215]

One of the most dramatic features of the case was the evidence from serving soldiers. Far from being the 'cream of the earth', in the mixed metaphor of the Devizes Major-General, these soldiers revealed in their evidence the enormous ignorance of their legal and political position which the BWNIC was designed, in part, to remedy. Two brothers from Cwmbran explained that when they had tried to leave the army they had received no help from the service, had then gone absent without leave, and had then both been court-martialled and were still in the army. Both denied that the leaflets had had any influence on them. A lance-corporal in the Royal Electrical and Mechanical Engineers stated that he had gone AWOL in June 1973, and had gone to Gwynneth Williams at BWNIC who 'had helped him to think for himself'. He had decided that 'what the army was doing in Northern Ireland was wrong', deserted to Sweden, and eventually returned to Britain where he gave himself up to court-martial. Guardsman Paul Machin, who gave evidence whilst serving nine-months detention in Colchester Military Prison, explained that he had also contacted Gwynneth Williams during his fourteen months of being AWOL, and that she had advised him to return to his unit.[216]

Several of the defendants conducted their own defence. For them, there was greater opportunity to exploit the leeway accorded by the court to the unrepresented, and hence of making more explicitly political statements. As Gwynneth Williams put it when the judge advised her to obtain legal advice: 'When it is my deepest beliefs which are on trial, no barrister, however brilliant, can properly represent me as I can myself'. Williams and the other defendants made a number of highly important political statements during the course of the trial, which demonstrably impressed the jury.[217]

One of the defendants who conducted his own defence, William Hetherington, also faced a charge under Section 1 of the 1934 Act of endeavouring to seduce a sailor, Stoker Woods, from his duty or allegiance during a conversation in a train from Swansea to Birmingham, and later in the waiting-room in Birmingham station. Hetherington was alleged to have explained to Woods about the then pending Old Bailey trial, and to have shown Woods a copy of *Peace News* describing the Lambeth committal proceedings. Woods reported the conversation to an officer.

In a summing-up which was not widely admired, Judge McKinnon made a number of factual errors about the defence case, and contributed very little new material for the student of the law. He explained that a person's religious beliefs and ideals could not be a defence if it was found that the law had been broken. He instructed the jury to ignore the argument that the Act was a bad law. At one point, Judge McKinnon sparked off a violent courtroom controversy when he broke an agreement with the defence that he would not mention matters of fact or opinion from Justice Lawton's summing-up of the Arrowsmith appeal of 1974. McKinnon quoted Lawton's view that 'this leaflet is the clearest incitement to mutiny', whereupon the defendants denounced this break of agreement, and explained that Justice Lawton had once been a candidate on behalf of the British Union of Fascists.[218]

The jury was sent out to consider their verdict at 11am on 10 December 1975. At 12.40pm they returned to announce unanimous not guilty verdicts on the 31 charges upon which they had to decide. 'This is a bad day for the country', Crown counsel was heard to remark. Williams, who had pleaded guilty to two Army Act charges, and Hyatt, who had similarly pleaded guilty to one, all under section 192(1), were fined £50 on each charge.[219] The result of the trial was front page news in the national press. The *Guardian* called the trial 'a rare glimpse of one of the British government's rawest nerves' and the verdict 'the clearest vindication yet of the growing body of critics who claim that the conspiracy laws and the Incitement to Disaffection Act have fallen into complete disrepute'. The *New Statesman* called it 'good news for the Labour movement . . . bad, indeed terminal, news for the Government's senior law officer, Mr Sam Silkin, who personally authorised the prosecution of the British Withdrawal from Northern Ireland 14'. The NCCL called for the repeal of the Act, and said, 'this result vindicates our campaign against the Incitement Act and we hope that it will go some way to preserve freedom of expression and to establish the rights of soldiers to information'. The Haldane Society similarly called for 'the speedy abolition' of 'this discredited legislation'.[220] Appropriately, because it had produced the most consistent, comprehensive reports on the case and the trial, it was left to *Peace News,* to sound a note of caution about the extent of the victory. 'Juries may side with us, but the law of the land is stacked against us', they stated, and continued:

> 'Boldly and right well as the 14 stood up for themselves in court, it's a fluke that they got off (if you can call it "getting off" – sitting through a 51-day trial, waiting for over a year between the charges and the verdicts). It isn't a fluke that the leaflet was acquitted – it was very carefully drafted – but there is little doubt that if we communicate with more soldiers more effectively, more of us will be punished'.[221]

As mentioned earlier, the original arrests of the fourteen BWNIC supporters sparked off a defence campaign, which was well documented through the columns of *Peace News.* A number of arrests followed, under the Incitement to Disaffection Act, of defence campaign supporters, who handed out the leaflets either as part of the BWNIC campaign, or as a show of solidarity with the original fourteen. The prosecuting authorities were obviously at this time in no doubt that the leaflet, 'Some Information for Discontented Soldiers', would if distributed establish grounds for Section 1 charges.

On 28 April 1975, Andrew Lloyd was charged under Section 2(1) of the 1934 Act for having possessed copies of the leaflet. He was reported to the police in December 1974 while distributing copies of the BWNIC leaflet addressed to civilians on a housing estate in Preston.

In 1974 this second leaflet addressed to civilians was sent by Aldershot MP, Julian Critchley, to the Defence Minister, Roy Mason, who apparently felt that it could be interpreted as encouraging people to help deserters and forwarded it to the DPP. No action was taken on the basis of that leaflet, then or when Andrew Lloyd was charged. At his committal proceedings in May 1975, however, much was made of it and prior to his trial in mid-September another common law charge of attempting to incite persons to contravene the 1934 Act was added; i.e. attempting to incite persons to endeavour to seduce members of the forces from their duty or allegiance. It was submitted that this charge, containing as it does three inchoate offences, was bad in law. This appears to have been accepted by the Judge. On the first charge under Section 2(1), the jury was unable to reach a unanimous verdict and the Judge was forced to order a retrial. On 5 January 1976, in the light of the Old Bailey verdict, the prosecution offered no evidence against Lloyd, and the case fell.[222]

One other interesting feature of this case was when Lloyd was originally reported to the police he was with a US citizen and because of this they also considered charging him with aiding and abetting an offence under Section 3(1) of the *Aliens Restriction (Amendment) Act* of 1919.

Late in April 1975, twelve members of the Cambridge University Liberal Club were questioned by the police in connection with their distribution of the 'Some Information for Discontented Soldiers' leaflet. Police had received a complaint from a member of the Officer Training Corps after he received a copy when one thousand were distributed in the Market Square in protest against the 1934 Act and the conspiracy laws. On 10 May, 200 people took part in a collective defiance of the Act in Cambridge. A member of the Liberal Party National Executive urged them all to distribute the leaflet even if it meant them breaking the law. (He was not charged.) They all walked to the nearby Army Recruiting Office and on finding it closed posted the leaflets through the letterbox; one police officer is reported to have helped in this. Three thousand leaflets were distributed and at about the same time 2,000 were distributed with the Cambridge *Broadsheet*. No action was taken, although the outcome of the earlier police investigations was that two people who had distributed the leaflet to members of the OTC were told by the police, apparently on behalf of the DPP, that if they promised not to repeat the action no proceedings would be taken. They did so promise.

On 29 May the *Guardian* published a letter from ten people, including three Professors (one of Law), two clergymen and a retired Brigadier, protesting against the 1934 Act and the above prosecutions and indicating that at 12.30pm on that day as many of them as possible would distribute 'Some Information for Discontented Soldiers' to soldiers in the Army Information Centre in Bradford. Six of them found the centre closed specially for the occasion and after pushing the leaflets under the door, accompanied an Inspector to the Police Station. They were told that reports would be sent to the DPP. No further action was taken.[223]

Other protests occurred. On 22 July, Ian Baird, Sandy Blake, Ross Bradshaw and Bill Stokes were arrested whilst handing out leaflets, including 'Some Information for Discontented Soldiers' at the Open Day of the Condor Royal Marines barracks at Arbroath, Scotland. They were charged under the Incitement to Disaffection Act, and bailed to appear before the sheriff court in Arbroath on 16 January 1976. However, when the Old Bailey verdict was reached, the prosecution was abandoned on the instruction of Mr Ronald King Murray, the Lord Advocate. This removed the possibility of an Incitement to Disaffection trial under Scottish law, something which has never yet occurred.[224]

Also in July 1975, six people were arrested in Platts Field, Manchester, during leafletting and street theatre against an army recruiting display which was a somewhat unlikely part of the annual Manchester Flower Show. Richard Bircumshaw, Sylvia Lerner, Stephen Minshull, Nicola Jeffs-Bedford, Andrew Sidwell and Susan Jones were arrested whilst performing what *Peace News* described as 'an impressive street play, showing the links between capitalism and the army and ending with a forceful portrayal of the British Army's role in Northern Ireland'. Charges were made of breach of the peace and incitement to disaffection, the latter on the basis of what their solicitor claimed was police planting of the 'Some Information for Discontented Soldiers' leaflet after the arrest of the street play. As in the Arbroath case, the Old Bailey result caused the prosecution to be dropped, on 6 January 1976.[225]

During the summer of 1975, there were other actions in support of the defendants, and in furtherance of the BWNI campaign. In July, soldiers in Inverness were leafletted, but no charges were made. On 16 August, about 30 people leafletted the Army's Armex 75 display at the Great Yorkshire Show in Harrogate; several of the demonstrators were detained, questioned and photographed by the police, but no charges were made, although there were threats of the use of the Incitement to Disaffection Act. 'Some Information for Discontented Soldiers' was regularly distributed by supporters in York during the summer. On 19 September, Young Liberals marched through Scarborough, handing out the leaflets and demanding the dropping of all charges under the Act. On 30 September, as the Old Bailey trial opened, four BWNIC members distributed the leaflets in Derry, after giving their names to the Royal Ulster Constabulary. No prosecutions were attempted in these cases.[226]

One other charge was brought in 1975. It arose out of a statement which was drafted and printed as part of a campaign against the prosecutions (see Appendix). It invited people possessing a copy of the leaflet and prepared to distribute it, to sign a statement to this effect. Over 500 people made this distinctive protest, and all the signatures were presented to the Home Secretary on the first morning of the Old Bailey trial.[227] One of the organisers of the 'statement of complicity', Alix Otten, was charged at Common Law with inciting others to commit an offence under the Incitement to Disaffection Act. Charges of inciting persons to contravene the 1797 Act occurred in several of the cases discussed above, but they are particularly objectionable in these areas since in these statuses an 'attempt' is made the substantive offence. Thus the charge against Alix Otten was of inciting others to endeavour to seduce members of the forces from their duty to allegiance *or* inciting others to possess or have under their control, with intent to aid, abet, counsel or procure the commission of an offence under Section 1, a document of such a nature that the dissemination of copies thereof among members of the forces would constitute such an offence.

The Otten case was heard by Stipendiary Magistrate John Bamber at Manchester Magistrates Court on 18 November 1975. The magistrate took great exception to the case against Otten, prepared by the Special Branch and the DPP. He attacked the prosecution for not stating when Otten had attempted to incite; he described 'Some Information for Discontented Soldiers' as 'hardly seductive – it contains some very good advice . . . eminently sensible'; he welcomed the absence of conspiracy charges, which were 'all too common these days'; he attacked the inclusion of references in police statements to the Lambeth committal of the fourteen BWNIC supporters because 'the reason why this statement has been included is to say that 14 people have already been committed for trial in connection with this leaflet, and would I kindly mind my own business and commit this defendant for trial'. The magistrate concluded his rumbustious and highly relevant destruction of the prosecution case by stating: 'She is not shown with sufficient certainty to have had certain documents under her control of such a nature that, if disseminated amongst members of HM Forces, might procure a breach of Section 1 of the Act. On that basis, I don't think it would be right to commit her for trial'.[228]

It is clear that an attempt to crush the British Withdrawal from Northern Ireland Campaign was systematically made during 1974 and 1975. This must have been done for a reason. The reason, presumably, was that the campaign did two important things; it threatened the impermeability of the military structure, and it appealed to a number of individuals whose morale was extremely low, and whose sense of helplessness in the intractible civil conflict in Ireland was increasing. Hence the link between the charges under the Incitement to Disaffection Act and those under the Army Act (Hyatt and Williams were not the only people charged in 1975 with aiding soldiers contrary to the Army Act). Very little information is available to the public and to the researcher concerning buyings-out by soldiers, and general army morale, but it is clear that the number of buyings-out have increased in the 1970s, and that there have been demonstrations among soldiers against further tours of duty in Northern Ireland. A *Midweek* BBC-1 television programme in late 1974 revealed that since the army had been sent into Northern Ireland in 1969, 787 soldiers had deserted and not returned. Self-evidently, the BWNIC prosecutions were no esoteric exercise in upholding an obscure law; they were a deliberate attempt to prevent the success of a tactic which effectively threatened the power of the military in this country. To the disbelief and puzzlement of many, they failed.

Conclusion

This study of the development of the incitement laws demonstrates that the paternalism of the British State towards the guardians of its stability has increased during the last 150 years. Wyndham's 1795 isolation of the armed forces and the *Incitement to Mutiny Act 1797* were both denounced at the time by those who believed a standing army to be unconstitutional, and who perceived the real danger of such a force being isolated from society at large, under the control of almost any government. Such policies and such laws are the final weapons of the state, ensuring civilian quiescence. Every development of the incitement laws up to the present day has been a logical progression from Wyndham's proposal to make the soldiery deaf by ensuring their physical isolation.

The unfaltering determination of successive executives and the military authorities from 1912 to 1934 to maintain and strengthen this isolation resulted in the *Incitement to Disaffection Act.* By widening the scope of the offences, the 1934 Act further restricted the freedom of speech and association of civilians, and further isolated the armed forces from political life. The constitutional principle that a soldier is a citizen was thus rendered an even greater illusion.[229] However, the persistence of the illusion has helped to disguise the reality of the situation, and has thus ensured that the degree of isolation, and the undemocratic internal structure of the armed forces have rarely been questioned. Indeed, the NCCL Conference in 1946 on Democratisation in the Forces is probably the only deep public discussion of the issues since 1934. The trade union movement has consistently neglected the denial of rights to servicemen, although earlier in the century this was a prime concern. Labour governments have done nothing to discourage this neglect.

The success of the anti-syndicalist prosecutions in 1912 proved that the 1797 *Incitement to Mutiny Act* was a powerful anti-working class weapon where it could be shown that workers were interfering with military independence. The danger in thus adapting statutes to new purposes in the political field has been shown by David Williams.[230] 'The courts are themselves put in an invidious position. They do not initiate or even encourage prosecutions. But they have to interpet the law, statutory and non statutory, as it stands. The prosecutions of 1834, 1912 and 1925 all left a legacy of suspicion as to the impartiality of the courts'.[231]

The anti-trade union character of this type of law is particularly obvious from the circumstances which led to the drafting of Section 3 of the *Police Act 1919,* and the embodiment in that law of the repression of a trade union. Fortunately, Trenchard's proposals for the militarisation of the police were not politically acceptable to the National Government, although some Cabinet Ministers clearly favoured them. The offence under Section 3 of the 1919 Act is arguably even more repressive than the *Incitement to Disaffection Act.* The police are physically integrated with the rest of society; if they are to perform the range of duties required of them they should be socially and politically integrated too. Yet the Section 3 offence, the scope of which is indicated by the two cases cited in the text, can only be used to erect barriers.

Once a political activity is controlled closely by the Criminal Law there is every danger that a reactionary state apparatus will extend it with greater ease than it could introduce it. In such a way, the *Defence of the Realm Regulations* presented the authorities with an experience of arbitrary power which served as a blueprint for permanent legislation in peacetime. The military authorities pressed constantly for this new law, until they secured it in 1934.

There is no doubt that many politicians in the period between 1917 and 1934 sincerely believed that a very grave danger was posed by Communists in Britain. In their view, the virulence of Communism could not be under-estimated, and they were convinced that this was due principally to CP-led and inspired trades unions. Convinced as they were that the militancy of the workers and the unemployed was due to Communist infiltration, they were horrified at the inadequate weapon to hand in the Criminal Law. The more that troops were used to aid the civil power against strikers and hunger-marchers, the more they were in contact with precisely those people from whom the authorities were most anxious to isolate them, and the more urgently new legislation was advocated. Ruling class attitudes were most clearly ventilated by Lord Hailsham, who stated in the 1934 House of Lords debate on the Incitement to Disaffection Bill that solders were never used in industrial disputes – only in preserving law and order.[232] Whereas the 1797 Act had been a product of specific political circumstances in its own time and had been adapted to meet the perceived needs of the political situation in 1912, so this new legislation was designed fundamentally to combat working-class propaganda which aimed at encouraging soldiers – workers in uniform – to see the way they were being employed to defeat industrial struggles. It is no surprise that the Incitement to Disaffection Bill was first recommended by the Cabinet Committee considering the hunger marches.

Perhaps the most seriously disturbing aspect of the history of the 1934 Act is the obscurantist and unswervingly hostile attitude of the Army Council not only to overtly communist propaganda (which one might at least expect), but also to any suggestion, however mild, in favour of democratisation of the armed forces. Dispelling the notion that the military leadership is 'ideologically uncommitted and uninvolved', Ralph Miliband has written:

It does not seem worth labouring the point that high-ranking officers in (advanced capitalist) countries have constituted a deeply conservative and even reactionary element in the state system and in society generally, and that their social origin, class situation and professional interest have led them to view the character and content of democratic politics with distaste, suspicion and hostility.[233]

And later, Miliband adds:

Given their whole ideological orientation, military and police elites may always be expected to support with particular zeal the determination of the civil power to combat 'internal subversion', particularly from the Left, and to act, particularly in times of social strife and open class conflict. These are the managers of that coercive function which is the State's prerogative; and in whatever other regards the civil power may at one time or another have entertained doubts as to their reliability, loyalty and subordination, it has hardly ever had occasion to have any serious doubts as to their readiness to take the field, so to speak, against striking workmen, left-wing political activists, and other such disturbers of the status quo.[234]

Immediately after the First World War, the military and police authorities did question the loyalty of the ranks and their readiness to act, but the direct consequence was the demand for greater power to control civilian propaganda. The military, though prone to paternalistic eulogies of the indomitable qualities of the ordinary soldiers on whom their power depends, have never been so sentimental as to neglect the reality of that power. For this reason, they have always taken precautions to protect soldiers from persuasion, to make certain that a cordon sanitaire of ignorance surrounds the loyalty of the ranks. The soldiers are not the only ones affected. Civilian freedom of speech is curtailed as a direct consequence.

The immediate effectiveness of the Army Council's pressure tactics was, nevertheless, due to exaggeration of the threat to State security. Both the army and the security services contributed to this process, the one feeding the other. Huntingdon has suggested that such groups have a predisposition to exaggerate threats.

The military man normally views with alarm the potency and immediacy of the security threats to the State – he recognises the continuing character of the threats to the State, but he also stresses the urgency of the current danger. The goal of professional competence requires the military man to estimate the threat as accurately as possible. But the military man also has a professional interest and a professional duty to stress the dangers to military security. Consequently the objective realities of international politics only partially determine the military estimate of the situation. The military man's views also reflect a subjective professional bias, the strength of which depends upon his general level of professionalism. This professional bias, or sense of professional responsibility, leads him to feel that if he errs in his estimate, it should be on the side of overstating the threat. Consequently, at times he will see threats to the security of the State where actually no threats exist.[235]

Huntingdon's somewhat apologetic tone cannot conceal the dangers of such exaggeration as he refers to, when it forms the basis of governmental policy and a legislative programme.

The passage of the *Incitement to Disaffection Act* must be one of the most blatant examples of executive deception in attempting to steer an innovatory measure through Parliament while proclaiming that it is an uncontroversial procedural Bill. Because the British Constitution is an unwritten one, it is vulnerable to surreptitious change at the hands of those who wield power in its name. The 1934 Act indicates just how easily it can be changed for the worse, and its passage remains a severe indictment of the excessive power of a coalition government ostensibly acting in the national interest.

Following his excellent account of the passage of the Bill, Professor Street quotes a leading textbook on Constitutional Law as saying that 'this measure arms the Government with a means of restricting the distribution of political propaganda; particularly it could be used to suppress the distribution of pacifist literature'.[236] He then questions this view, and, reminding the reader that there is no law against the distribution of political propaganda unless the intent to seduce servicemen is proved, reaches the astounding conclusion that:

although the original Bill conferred unreasonably wide powers on the Executive to interfere with the citizen, the Act, despite some objectionable features, is not now a serious threat to liberty. Indeed, this account of the passage of the Bill through Parliament furnishes an excellent example of the way in which Parliament can operate effectively as a watchdog of liberty.[237]

Granted, opposition to the Bill forced the Government to make several important concessions, but it was undoubtedly the crucial role of the opposition outside Parliament which was most effective in this regard. The point which Street neglects is that in 1934 Parliament was prevented, by the unique excessive power of the National Government, from acting in any way as a watchdog of liberty. Rushed illiberal legislation is not in any way the absolute prerogative of National Governments – the recent *Prevention of Terrorism (Temporary Provisions) Act* is a case in point – but the particular character of the National Government's political majority was a decisive factor in encouraging the tabling of the Incitement to Disaffection Bill, and in ensuring its passage in the face of sustained eloquent opposition.

This study should have demonstrated the wrongness of Street's denial of the existence of any law against political propaganda. This claim has been made during each prosecution under the 1797 and the 1934 Acts; rebuttal of it has been a central part of the defence of each of the cases. It has to be admitted, of course, that when statutory wording is as vague and all-embracing as it is in this legislation, its scope in practice will depend upon the ease with which the authorities feel that prosecutions can be successfully brought, rather than upon the zealous prosecution of each and every publication which might be tested under the Act.

There is nothing new in the notion of Executive interference in the administration of justice. However, as the evidence of it is rarely contemploraneous with the accusation, the myth of Executive non-interference remains, albeit somewhat tarnished. Sir Arthur Irvine, a former Labour Law Officer under Harold Wilson, has said that the Prime Minister 'did not initiate or permit any interference with the Law Officers' responsibilities . . . Indeed . . . he never allowed any Cabinet discussion of a matter involving possible legal action by the law officers in their capacities as officers of the Crown'.[238] It is therefore ironic that this policy, hypocritical in its purism, may well be absolutely disastrous, and more so than if consultation were admitted and open. If the Attorney-General of 1974, Samuel Silkin, and the DPP, Sir Norman Skelhorn, initiated the prosecutions against the BWNI Campaign purely on their own decision, without any Cabinet responsibility, then they might have learned from the caution of certain of their predecessors, who showed less regard for the letter of the law. One feature of many of the earlier prosecutions discussed above was the restraint shown by the Executive in the initiation of proceedings. This restraint was due, not so much to the nature of the evidence, as to the political timing of the prosecution. As this study has shown, the authorities are sometimes unwilling to warn that a particular activity may be contrary to a particular statute because their primary concern is less with the criminality of an individual, more with the political problem posed by a movement or organisation. Even more objectionable is the extension of this policy through the use of agents provocateurs to entrap people into 'political crime'.

Another leading textbook on Constitutional Law also notes that the 1934 Act could be used 'against persons distributing pacifist literature to members of the Forces'. The author continues, 'in this area of the law, restraint in instituting proceedings, the prospect of a restrictive direction by a judge and an acquittal by a jury are the effective safeguards for the expression of political dissent'.[239] The present study hardly justifies faith in these safeguards. From 1974-6, Attorney-General Silkin and DPP Skelhorn showed great lack of restraint in instituting proceedings; Mr Justice Abdela, and Judge McKinnon certainly gave no restrictive directions as to the law; the acquittal of the fourteen BWNIC supporters in December 1975 does not represent a safeguard against the repression of future political dissent, even of the BWNIC type.

The failure of the Crown to convince twelve jury members that the BWNIC supporters had contravened the *Incitement to Disaffection Act* has been hailed in diverse ways. It is clearly seen by many as a victory for civil liberties. Others see it as vindicating the importance of jury trial in the face of attack on that institution from the police. Some would argue that the acquittal shows the safeguards against injustice in the British system, and that criticism of the Act is therefore largely irrelevant. Finally, there will be those who conclude that the law is in desperate need of being strengthened.

The breadth of the Act is in no way affected by the acquittal. Obviously, the very prompt acquittal after a 51-day trial which cost some £250,000 is an indictment of the judgement of those responsible for the prosecutions, but it would be inaccurate to characterise it as anything more than a very limited victory for civil liberties. The Act itself still exists, and no point of law was established in the 1975 trials which even mitigates its sweeping applicability. It would therefore be unwise, even irresponsible, for those who have campaigned against the Act, against the prosecutions, and against the things which they represent, to cease on account of the acquittals.

At the trial of Pat Arrowsmith, much was made of the introductory and concluding paragraphs of the original BWNIC leaflet. Lord Justice Lawton said in the Appeal hearing that the argument that it was purely informative was an insult to the intelligence of the jury. Admittedly, the tone of the document changed considerably in the redrafting, but in retrospect the idea that redrafting would secure immunity from prosecution, as distinct from conviction, seems naive. What concerned the authorities was not so much the content of the document (though this was relevant) as the fact that the documents were being made available at all.

If freedom of speech and communication is to be a meaningful concept, the repeal of the *Incitement to Disaffection Act,* and the relevant sections of the *Police Act* and the *Aliens Restriction (Amendment) Act* would obviously be of great importance. The offences under the *Incitement to Mutiny Act* requiring endeavour to seduce from duty *and* allegiance are more than sufficient for the protection of the State. A real endeavour to seduce from duty *and* allegiance would obviously be very serious, and there is thus less need for the summary procedure provisions. Having said this, it is inconceivable that the remaining provisions would be anything other than repressive of free speech unless certain fundamental internal changes are made within the armed forces. This complex subject is outside the scope of this study, but any attempt to reconstruct the incitement laws which fails to accommodate the basic provocation to 'incitement' – the making of political and industrial demands within the armed forces – would fail to eradicate the problem. This is something of which the trades unions will be conscious when there is any legislative enactment of the Law Commission's as yet unwritten report on treason and related offences. Free speech and association in the armed forces may then be made distinct from mutiny or disaffection.

It may be argued that civilians have no right to interfere with the control over the armed forces exercised by a democratically elected government. It is at times of crisis, when governments tend to forget their democratic basis, when the military and police exceed their normal duties and create a new normality, when liberal policies are most at stake, that this area of the law is most likely to be revived. At such times there is less restraint in the instituting of proceedings, less likelihood of careful directions on law from the judges, less chance of acquittals by jury. In a democracy, the validity of justice should not depend upon circumstances. Neither actual nor (perhaps more important) perceived crises should interfere with the basic freedoms except in the most extreme circumstances, and then only after very careful consideration and general acceptance of the need. As presently drafted and conceived none of the legislation with which this study is concerned satisfies these criteria.

Appendix I

THE INCITEMENT TO DISAFFECTION ACT 1934
(24 & 25 Geo.5.c.56)

1. Penalty on persons endeavouring to seduce members of his Majesty's forces from their duty or allegiance.
If any person maliciously and advisedly endeavours to seduce any member of His Majesty's forces from his duty or allegiance to His Majesty, he shall be guilty of an offence under this Act.

2. Provisions for the prevention and detection of offences under this Act
(1) If any person, with intent to commit or to aid, abet, counsel, or procure the commission of an offence under section one of this Act, has in his possession or under his control any document of such a nature that the dissemination of copies thereof among members of His Majesty's forces would constitute such an offence, he shall be guilty of an offence under this Act.

(2) If a judge of the High Court is satisfied by information on oath that there is reasonable ground for suspecting that an offence under this Act has been committed, and that evidence of the commission thereof is to be found at any premises or place specified in the information, he may, on an application made by an officer of police of a rank not lower than that of inspector, grant a search warrant authorising any such officer as aforesaid named in the warrant together with any other persons named in the warrant and any other officers of police to enter the premises or place at any time within one month from the date of the warrant, if necessary by force, and to search the premises or place and every person found therein, and to seize anything found on the premises or place or on any such person which the officer has reasonable ground for suspecting to be evidence of the commission of such an offence as aforesaid:

Provided that –

(a) a search warrant shall only be issued in respect of an offence suspected to have been committed within the three months prior to the laying of the information thereof; and (b)if a search warrant under this Act has been executed on any premises, it shall be the duty of the officer of the police who has conducted or directed the search to notify the occupier that the search has taken place, and to supply him with a list of any documents or other objects which have been removed from the premises, and where any documents have been removed from any other person to supply that person with a list of such documents.

(3) No woman shall, in pursuance of a warrant issued under the last foregoing subsection, be searched except by a woman.

(4) Anything seized under this section may be retained for a period not exceeding one month, or if within that period proceedings are commenced for an offence under this Act until the conclusion of those proceedings, and, in relation to property which has come into the possession of the police under this section, the Police (Property) Act 1897 (which makes provision with respect to the disposal of property in the possession of the police) shall have effect subject to the foregoing provisions of this subsection and to the provisions of this Act concerring powers on courts dealing with offences.

3. Provisions as to punishment of offences

(1) A person guilty of an offence under this Act shall be liable, on conviction on indictment to imprisonment for a term not exceeding two years or to a fine not exceeding four months or to a fine not exceeding two hundred pounds, or on summary conviction to imprisonment for a term not exceeding four months or to a fine not exceeding twenty pounds, or (whether on conviction on indictment or on summary conviction) to both such imprisonment and fine.

(2) No prosecution in England under this Act shall take place without the consent of the Director of Public Prosecutions.

(3) Where a prosecution under this Act is being carried on by the Director of Public Prosecutions, a court of summary jurisidiction shall not deal with the case summarily without the consent of the Director.

(4) Where any person is convicted of an offence under this Act, the court dealing with the case may order any documents connected with the offence to be destroyed or dealt with in such other manner as may be specified in the order, but no documents shall be destroyed before the expiration of the period within which an appeal may be lodged, and if an appeal is lodged no document shall be destroyed until after the appeal has been heard and decided.

4. Short title and application to Scotland and Northern Ireland

(1) This Act may be cited as the Incitement to Disaffection Act, 1934.

(2) This Act shall apply to Scotland subject to the following modifications:—

(a) subsection (2) of section two shall have effect as if for references to a judge of the High Court there were substituted references to the sheriff, and any application for a search warrant under the said subsection shall be made by the procurator fiscal instead of such officer as is therein mentioned;

(b) subsection (4) of section two shall not apply provided that anything seized under that section may be retained for a period not exceeding one month, or if within that period proceedings are commenced for an offence under this Act until the conclusion of those proceedings, and subject as aforesaid and to the provisions of any enactment, including this Act, conferring powers on courts dealing with offences, any property which has come into the hands of the police under this section shall be returned to the owner, or, if the owner cannot be ascertained, shall be disposed of in such a manner as the sheriff, in a summary application made to him, may direct;

(c) the powers conferred by this Act on the sheriff shall not be exercised by an honorary sheriff substitute.

(3) It is hereby declared that this Act extends to Northern Ireland, and in the application thereof to Northern Ireland the provisions of this Act requiring the consent of the Director of Public Prosecutions to the summary trial of cases shall have effect as if references to the Attorney-General for Northern Ireland were therein substituted for references to the Director of Public Prosecutions.

Appendix II

OPEN LETTER TO BRITISH SOLDIERS

Men! Comrades! Brothers!
You are in the army.
So are we. You, in the army of Destruction. We, in the Industrial, or army of Construction.

We work at mine, mill, forge factory or dock etc., producing and transporting all the goods, clothing, stuffs etc., which makes it possible for people to live.

You are Workingmen's sons.

When We go on strike to better our lot, which is the lot also of Your Fathers, Mothers, Brothers and Sisters, You are called upon by your Officers to MURDER US.

Don't do it.

You know how it happens. Always has happened.

We stand out as long as we can. Then one of our (and your) irresponsible Brothers, goaded by the sight and thought of his and his loved ones' misery and hunger, commits a crime on property. Immediately you are ordered to murder Us, as You did at Mitchelstown, at Featherstone, at Belfast.

Don't You Know, that when you are out of the colours, and become a 'Civvy' again, that You, like Us, may be on strike, and You, like Us, be liable to be murdered by other soldiers.

Boys, Don't Do it.

'Thou shalt not kill', says the Book.

Don't forget that!

It does not say 'unless you have a uniform on'.

No! MURDER IS MURDER, whether committed in the heat of anger on one who has wronged a loved one, or by clay-piped Tommies with a rifle.

Boys, Don't do it.

Act the Man! Act the Brother! Act the Human being!

Property can be replaced! Human Life, Never!

The Idle Rich Class, who own and order you about, own and order us about also. They and their friends own the land, and the means of life in Britain.

You Don't! We Don't!

When We kick they order You to murder Us.

When You kick, You get court-martialled and cells.

Your fight is Our fight. Instead of fighting Against each other We should be fighting with each other.

Out of Our loins, Our lives, Our homes, You come.

Don't disgrace Your Parents, Your Class, by being the willing tools any longer of the Master Class.

You, like Us, are of the Slave Class. When We rise, You rise; When We fall, even by your bullets, Ye fall also. England with its fertile valleys and dells, its mineral resources, its sea harvests, is a heritage of ages to us.

You have no doubt joined the army out of poverty. We work long hours for small wages at hard work, because of our poverty. And both Your poverty and Ours arises from the fact that, Britain with its resources, belongs to only a few people. These few, owning Britain, own Our jobs. Owning Our jobs they own Our very lives. Comrades, have we called in vain? Think things out and refuse any longer to Murder your Kindred. Help US to win back Britain for the British, and the World for the Workers.

[This appeal gave rise to the Syndicalist prosecutions of 1912. It was printed in *The Syndicalist* of January 1912.]

Appendix III

THE ARMY AND INDUSTRIAL DISPUTES – AN OPEN LETTER TO THE FIGHTING FORCES

Comrades,

You never joined the Army or Navy because you were in love with warfare, or because you were attracted by the glamour of the uniform. In nine cases out of ten you were compelled to join the services after a long fight against poverty and misery caused by prolonged unemployment.

Once in the services, you are subjected to a military discipline that bears down upon you in an ever-increasing manner.

Repressive regulations and irksome restrictions are intentionally imposed upon you. And when war is declared you are supposed to be filled with a longing to 'beat the enemy'. The enemy consists of working men like yourselves, living under the same slave conditions. But the Government not only organises the services for war, it also keeps them fully equipped to be able to crush their own workers when the need arises.

Have you noticed how, in large strikes and lock-outs, all the newspapers condemn the strikers, and talk about maintaining the 'essential services and the food supplies'? Have you forgotten that during the Tonypandy strike of railway men in 1911, the soldiers were used and workers were shot? That gunboats were used by Asquith to defeat the dockers in 1912? Have you forgotten how the Labour Government threatened to use naval men during the dockers' strike this year? How in the Tramway strike the Government threatened to introduce EPA, which would have forced many of you to have shot your own brothers and fathers? Have you forgotten the miners' lock-out in 1921, when the Reserves were called out, and Hyde Park was turned into a military camp in order that a large section of the Army could be ready to suppress any action that might take place as a result of the Triple Alliance strike?

Soldiers, sailors, airmen, flesh of our flesh and bone of our bone, the Communist Party calls upon you to begin the task of not only organising passive resistance when war is declared, or when an industrial dispute involves you, but to definitely and categorically let it be known that, neither in the class war nor a military war, will you turn your guns on your fellow workers, but instead will line up with your fellow workers in an attack upon the exploiters and capitalists, and will use your arms on the side of your own class.

Form Committees in every barracks, aerodrome and ship. Let this be the nucleus of an organisation that will prepare the whole of the soldiers, sailors and airmen, not merely to refuse to go to war, or to refuse to shoot strikers during industrial disputes, but will make it possible for the workers, peasants and soldiers, sailors and airmen to go forward in a common attack upon the capitalists, and smash capitalism for ever, and institute the reign of the whole working-class.

Refuse to shoot down your fellow workers!

Refuse to fight for profits!

Turn your weapons on your oppressors!

[This article gave rise to the 'Campbell Case' of 1924. It was printed in the *Workers' Weekly* of 25 July 1924.]

Appendix IV

SOME INFORMATION FOR DISCONTENTED SOLDIERS

This information has been compiled by supporters of the British Withdrawal from Northern Ireland Campaign who hope that it will be of some use to soldiers who have decided not to go to Northern Ireland. We are not recommending any particular course of action. There is no easy way out of the Army, but we hope that by one means or another you will avoid taking part in the killing in Northern Ireland.

IF YOU ARE A CONSCIENTIOUS OBJECTOR
that is, if since joining up you have developed a religious or moral objection to taking part in any war, you have a legal right to be discharged on these grounds.
– you are advised to contact:
The Central Board for Conscientious Objectors, c/o 6 Endsleigh Street, London WC1. Tel: 01-352 7906.

This organisation publishes a step-by-step guide to procedure for application for a discharge on grounds of conscience. Members also offer individual advice and support throughout the whole process and have considerable experience in giving this form of help.

IF YOU INTEND TO APPLY FOR A DISCHARGE ON OTHER GROUNDS
the following organisations may be able to help:
AT EASE, c/o Release, 1 Elgin Avenue, London W9. Tel: 01-837 9794.

'At Ease' was recently opened to deal with enquiries about all legal ways of leaving the armed forces.
Counsellors (who include ex-servicemen) are available at this address every Thursday evening from 7.30 to 9.30 pm. The help of sympathetic lawyers and social workers can be obtained if necessary. Advice is confidential. No representations will be made to anyone without your permission. No pressure will be applied, whatever you decide to do. 'At Ease' also deals with enquiries by post.
If it is impossible for you to call in person, 'At Ease' can sometimes

arrange for preliminary counselling to be given near to where you are based.

THE NATIONAL COUNCIL FOR CIVIL LIBERTIES,
186 Kings Cross Road, London WC1. Tel: 01-278 4575
Open daily – office hours.

This organisation has considerable experience in giving legal advice to servicemen and representing them to military authorities.

IF YOU HOPE THE ARMY WILL DISCHARGE YOU

– on political grounds, you may be interested in the wide selection of peace literature from:

The Peace Centre, 18 Moor Street Ringway, Birmingham 4. Tel: 021-643 0996

Housman's Bookshop, 5 Caledonian Road, London N1. Tel: 01-837 4473

– on sexual grounds, you may wish to contact:

The Campaign for Homosexual Equality, National Office, 28 Kennedy Street, Manchester 2, or their London Information Centre, *22 Great Windmill Street, London W1. Tel: 01-437 7363. Open from 6pm.* or phone *Icebreakers, 01-274 9590 from 7.30pm to 10.30pm.*

– on health grounds, we would advise you not to mutilate yourself, feign mental illness or take dangerous drugs. Some soldiers are doing so in desperation. If you have a genuine health problem, contact 'At Ease' (address above).

IF YOU HAVE DECIDED TO GO ABSENT WITHOUT LEAVE

– to Sweden, you will be pleased to know that special arrangements have been made to welcome British servicemen who go AWOL to Sweden by:

The British Deserters Support Group, c/o Bok-Cafe morianen, Box 16037, Drottninggatan 19, 103 21 Stockholm 16, Sweden. Tel: Stockholm 106063

If you go to Sweden, you will need your passport, your military ID card and about £30 cash (you need this to get through passport control as a tourist). You are advised to enter via Stockholm and avoid Malmo and Goteborg, and to enter as tourist.

You will need to wait three weeks before going to register with the police as an applicant for political asylum. If you contact the British

Deserters Support Group, they will put you in touch with a good Swedish lawyer, advise you on registration procedure, offer you accommodation with sympathetic Swedish people during the difficult three-week waiting period, and accompany you when you go to register with the police.

It is important to make it clear to the Swedish police that you were going to have to serve in Northern Ireland, otherwise you will not be considered for asylum. After you have registered, you can then go to the Swedish Social Bureau which will get you a place to stay, give you money to live on and help you to enrol in Swedish language classes.

A British AWOL soldier can apply for the type of asylum that has been granted to American and Portuguese AWOL soldiers. It amounts to the Swedish Government giving a man permission to stay on the basis of special circumstances – a type of humanitarian asylum. However, when you go to the police, you are advised to ask for political asylum so as to make sure that the Aliens Commission and not the police makes the final decision on your case.

Once you have permission to stay, you would have the right to work or study in Sweden and your wife and children could join you. Sweden has excellent educational and social services. There are facilities at Swedish Folk High Schools for men who wish to gain further qualifications or technical training. However, permission to stay is renewable every six months and the Swedish Government reserves the right to withdraw permission if you commit an offence. Some American, Portuguese and British AWOL soldiers have settled in Sweden. Some have found the difficulties of learning a new language and living as an immigrant in a new country too great. If you do decide to seek asylum, you are going into exile, so think it over carefully before you make an irrevocable decision.

– to Eire, you should know that this destination has proved to be dangerous for some British AWOL soldiers. Your situation may be exploited by violent extremist groups.
– to other countries, you should know that groups in the Netherlands, Germany and Switzerland are trying to help British AWOL soldiers but if apprehended in any of these countries, you are liable to be returned to the British authorities.
– in Britain, you may have difficulties over employment (no insurance cards) and accommodation (anyone who shelters you is liable to prosecution). You may have to keep moving to avoid arrest. If you are considering going AWOL in Britain, you should therefore plan ahead very carefully.

IF YOU INTEND TO REFUSE TO GO TO NORTHERN IRELAND you are likely to be court-martialled. You are entitled to be represented by a civilian lawyer if you so choose.

The National Council for Civil Liberties or *At Ease* (addresses above) will advise on a good one who is sympathetic to your position.

If you wish your action to be publicised, so as to set an example to other soldiers, strengthening their resolve to resist the Government's policy, then please contact the British Withdrawal from Northern Ireland Campaign (address below). Note: if a group of soldiers made this announcement simultaneously it would make a great impact on public opinion, both inside and outside the Army. Such an action could lead to Court Martial and imprisonment. But if you believe, as we do, that it is wrong for troops to be in Northern Ireland, we ask you to consider whether it is better to be killed for a cause you do not believe in or to be imprisoned for refusing to take part in the conflict. The opposition of American servicemen forced partial withdrawal from the war in Indochina. The Algerian war came to an end partly because it was opposed by hundreds of thousands of Frenchmen including soldiers, who refused to take part in it. British soldiers could save lives in Northern Ireland – not only their own lives.

The organisations listed above do not necessarily support the objectives of this Campaign and are not responsible for their inclusion in this document.

The entire responsibility for the production and distribution of this leaflet is that of

THE BRITISH WITHDRAWAL FROM NORTHERN IRELAND CAMPAIGN

c/o 5 Caledonian Road, London N1, England.

[This leaflet was the object of prosecutions in 1975, described in the final Chapters.]

Footnotes

1. *Cobbett's Parliamentary History of England* vol 32, col 935.
2. *ibid* vol 33, col 796
3 *ibid* vol 33, col 807
4 *ibid* vol 33, col 810
5 James Stephen: *A History of the Criminal Law of England* (London, 1883) p.294
6 *Hume on Crimes* (Edinburgh, 1819) vol i, p 520.
7 *Cobbett's Parliamentary History of England* vol 33, col 811
8 *ibid* vol 33, col 807
9 *ibid* vol 33, col 806
10 *37 Geo III c.70* (Incitement to Mutiny Act 1797)
11 Stephen: *op cit* p 294
12 *Cobbett's Parliamentary History of England* vol 35, col 901
13 G.D.H. Cole & Raymond Postgate: *The Common People 1746-1946* (London, 1963) p 450
14 *The Times* 1 March 1912
15 *ibid* 11 March 1912, 18 March 1912
16 *ibid* 22 March 1912, 29 March 1912. See also Tom Mann: *Memoirs* (London, 1967) pp 230-63
17 *The Times* 23 March 1912
18 *Parliamentary Debates (Commons)* (henceforth *Hansard*) 25 March 1912. Mann: *op cit* pp 238-49
19 *The Times* 10 May 1912
20 *ibid* 19 June 1912
21 *Hansard* 23 March 1914
22 A Barrister (D.N. Pritt): *Justice in England* (London, 1938) pp 221-7
23 *Manual of Emergency Legislation,* Suppl. 2-3, (1914-5) p 619
24 *Defence of the Realm Manual* (8th ed.) (1919) p 154
25 *Manual of Emergency Legislation,* Suppl.4 (1915) p 137
26 Charles Loch Mowat: *Britain Between the Wars* (London, 1955) p 5
27 V.L. Allen: 'The National Union of Police and Prison Officers': *Economic History Review* vol XI no 1 (1958)
28 General Sir N. Macready: *Annals of an Active Life* (London, 1924) vol II p 301
29 *ibid* p 356
30 *ibid* p 312
31 *loc cit*
32 *ibid* p 345
33 *ibid* p 352
34 *The Times* 4 August 1919
35 *Hansard* v.118 c.795
36 *ibid* cc.1577-88
37 A.J.P. Taylor: *English History 1914-45* (london, 1965) p 187
38 W.H. Crook: *The General Strike* (London, 1931) pp 240-3
39 quoted further in Crook: *op cit*
40 War Office (WO) 32-3948: 105/Gen/2736
41 *loc cit*
42 *Hansard* v.114 c.1246
43 WO 32-3948: 105/Gen/2871
44 Cabinet Papers (CP) 344(24) appendix
45 WO 32-3948: 105/Gen/2871
46 CP 544(20)

47 CP 703 (20)
48 Cab. 23/20 and WO 32-3948: 5/Bills/1873
49 Ralph Miliband: *Parliamentary Socialism* (London, 1972) pp 76-82
50 Cab. 23/20
51 Home Affairs Committee (HAC) (21), 86th conclusion, para 2.
52 Mowat: *op cit* p 121
53 HAC (21) 87th conclusion
54 WO 32-3948: 5/Bills/1873
55 *ibid*
56 S. Bowes: *The Police and Civil Liberties* (London, 1967) passim.
57 Wal Hannington: *Unemployed Struggles 1919-1936* (London, 1936) p 67
58 *ibid*
59 WO 32-3948: 5/Bills/2259
60 *Hansard* v.162, cc.1533-58. Also James Klugmann: *History of the Communist Party of Great Britain* (London, 1968) v.I, p 275.
61 *Hansard* v.171, cc.2319-20. Also Miliband: *op cit,* p 111.
62 CP 3010 (21)
63 CP 5 (24), CP 21 (24). Cf. Klugmann: *op cit* v.I pp 313-24
64 CP 273 (24)
65 Klugmann: *op cit* v.I pp 275-7
66 CP 230 (240)
67 Cabinet Conclusion 37 (24); CP 344 (24)
68 See Taylor: *op cit* p 275; Miliband: *op cit* p109
69 L.J. Macfarlane: *The British Communist Party* (London, 1966) p 106
70 R.W. Lyman: *The First Labour Government* (London, 1957) p 237
71 N.D. Siederer: 'The Campbell Case': *Journal of Contemporary History* v.9 no.2 (1974).
72 Macfarlane: *op cit* p106
73 Cabinet Conclusion 48 (24)
74 Thomas Jones: *Whitehall Diary* (ed. Keith Middlemass) (London, 1969) vol I, pp 290, 296.
75 Cabinet Conclusions 52 (24) 1.
76 D.N. Pritt: *Autobiography* (London, 1965) v.I p 21. For an extensive discussion of the relationship between the Attorney-General and the Executive, see L.J. Edwards: *The Law Officers of the Crown* (London, 1964).
77 Mowat: *op cit* p 182
78 W.P. and Z. Coates: *A History of Anglo-Soviet Relations* (London, 1943) chapter 8. Also Lyman: *op cit* pp 286-9.
79 WO 32-3948: 5/Bills/1873
80 Henry Pelling: *The British Communist Party* (London, 1958) p 32
81 Cabinet Conclusion 65 (24) 8
82 CP 544 (24)
83 Edwards: *op cit* pp 197-8
84 CP 544 (24). Edwards: *op cit* p 209
85 WO 32-3948: 110/Gen/3996
86 *ibid*
87 WO 32-3948: 110/Gen/3991
88 WO 32-3948: 110/Gen/3996
89 *ibid*
90 *ibid*
91 *ibid*
92 Cabinet Conclusion 47 (25) 2
93 VP 420 (25)
94 Cabinet Conclusion 48 (25) 2A
95 Hannington: *op cit* ch.VII. Harry Pollitt: *Serving my Time* (London, 1940) pp 209-48
96 A Barrister (D.N. Pritt): *op cit* p 219
97 *The Times,* 29 October 1925
98 *Parliamentary Papers* (1926) xxii, Cmnd. 2682, (Communist Papers) pp 583-743

99 Public Order Committee (POC) 25
100 Cabinet Conclusion 14 (26) 1
101 CP 136 (26)
102 *ibid*
103 WO 32-3948: 110/Gen/4063
104 WO 32-3948: 110/Gen/4036
105 *The Times,* 23 April 1954
106 Crook: *op cit* p 337
107 R.Page Arnot: *The General Strike* (London, 1926) p 189
108 Pelling: *op cit* p 36
109 *Edinburgh Evening News,* 13 June 1928; *The Times,* 29 June 1928
110 WO 32-3948: 110/Gen/4399
111 *ibid*
112 *ibid*
113 *ibid*
114 *ibid*
115 *Daily Worker,* 5 January 1931, 7 January 1931, 23 January 1931, 24 June 1931, 9 July 1931
116 *ibid,* 11 May 1931, 12 May 1931, 19 May 1931, 20 July 1931, 21 July 1931
117 Mowat: *op cit* p 402
118 *ibid* pp 403-6. Len Wincott: *Invergordon Mutineer* (London, 1974) passim
119 Cabinet Conclusion 56 (31) 5
120 Mowat: *op cit* p 406
121 CP 23/9013 folios 32-7
122 *ibid*
123 Pelling: *op cit* p67
124 Bowes: *op cit* p110
125 *The Times,* 28 September 1931, 3 October 1931
126 *ibid* 22 October 1931
127 *loc cit*
128 *ibid* 24 November 1931
129 Wincott: *op cit* p 138
130 *The Times* 17 October 1931. J. Curtis: *The Land of Liberty* (London, 1938) pp 97-9
131 *The Times* 3 October 1931
132 *ibid* 17 October 1931
133 *ibid* 27 November 1931
134 *ibid* 26 October 1931, 3 October 1931
135 Curtis: *op cit* p 99
136 WO 32-3948: 110/Gen/4638
137 *ibid*
138 *ibid*
139 WO 32-3948: 110/Gen/4771
140 Pelling: *op cit* p 72, for example.
141 WO 32-3948: 110/Gen/4771
142 *ibid*
143 Hannington: *op cit* passim
144 quoted *ibid* p 251 (from the 'Police Review')
145 *ibid* pp 254-66
146 *ibid* p 255
147 CP 434 (32)
148 Cabinet Conclusion 68 (32) 10; Cab 27/497
149 CP 60 (33)
150 Cabinet Conclusion 64 (31) 3
151 CP 60 (33)
152 *ibid*
153 *The Times* 31 January 1933
154 Pritt: *op cit* v.I p 140
155 *The Times:* 11 February 1933
156 Pritt: *op cit* v.I p 142

157 Curtis: *op cit* p 99
158 WO 32-3948: 110/Gen/4771
159 CP 230 (33)
160 Cabinet Conclusion 52 (33) 4
161 Cabinet Conclusion 53 (33) 6
162 WO 32-3948: 110/Gen/4771
163 CP 53 (34): CP 62 (34)
164 Cabinet Conclusion 8 (34) 6
165 *ibid*
166 WO 32-3948: 110/Gen/4771
167 *Hansard* v.288 c.743
168 NCCL Archives 1:2/1
169 NCCL Archives 1:75/5 (Notes of deputation by Treasury Reporter)
170 *The Spectator* 29 June 1934
171 *The Sedition Bill Exposed* (Communist Party) (London, 1934) p 15
172 *Law Journal* 12 May 1934
173 *Army, Navy and Air Force Gazette* (1934) v.75 p 895
174 Curtis: *op cit* p 36
175 W. Ivor Jennings: *The Sedition Bill Explained* (London, 1934). MacColl and Wells: 'The Incitement to Disaffection Bill': *Political Quarterly* (1934), 352.
176 *Hansard* v.288, c.740
177 *ibid* v.293 cc.201-33
178 CP 230 (33)
179 1765, 19 State Trials, 1030 at 1073
180 *ibid* 1063
181 *PP* Standing Committee A, Official Reports, 14 June 1934, c.243
182 1765, 19 State Trials, 1030 at 1066
183 *The Times* 18 November 1925
184 *op cit* 19 November 1925
185 *Hansard* v.118 c.2076
186 *Report of the Royal Commission on Police Powers and Procedure* (1929), para. 120
187 Pritt: *op cit* v.I p 139
188 *New Statesman* 21 April 1934
189 Ronald Kidd: *British Liberty in Danger* (London, 1940) pp 56-58
190 *ibid* p 37. *News Chronicle* 13 March 1937
191 Kidd: *op cit* p 196ff.
192 *ibid* p 216
193 *The Times* 7 June 1940. *Daily Telegraph* 7 June 1940
194 *The Times* 22 June 1940
195 *Kentish Mercury* 26 July 1940
196 *Jewish Chronicle* 25 February 1940
197 *Peace News* 25 August 1944
198 *Civil Liberty* June 1940
199 *Wildcat* no 1 (1974)
200 *New Statesman* 3 March 1951
201 *Peace News* 8 December 1972
202 *The Times* 25 January 1972
203 *Peace News* 31 August 1974. Larry Grant: 'The Controversial Act of 1934 and the Trial of Pat Arrowsmith': *Index* v.3 no.3 (Autumn 1974)
204 *Peace News* 24 May 1974, 7 June 1974
205 *ibid* 24 May 1974
206 *R v Arrowsmith* [1975] I All ER 463, [1975] 2 WLR 484
207 *The Times* 11 January 1972
208 *Peace News* 18 October 1974
209 Geoff Robertson: *Whose Conspiracy?* (London, 1974) (NCCL). Robert Hazell: *Conspiracy and Civil Liberties* (London, 1974) (Cobden Trust).
210 *The Guardian* 1 October 1975, 2 October 1975
211 see for instance *Socialist Worker* 27 September 1975

212 *The Times* 10 October 1975, *Morning Star* 10 October 1975
213 *The Kilburn Times* 21 November 1975
214 *The Guardian* 3 October 1975
215 *Peace News* 19 December 1975
216 *The Guardian* 13 October 1975, 23 October 1975, *Peace News* 21 November 1975
217 *Peace News* 21 November 1975, *The Guardian* 1 October 1975
218 *Peace News* 19 December 1975
219 *ibid*
220 *The Guardian* 11 December 1975, *New Statesman* 12 December 1975, *Morning Star,* 11 December 1975
221 *Peace News* 19 December 1975
222 *ibid* 27 June 1975, *The Guardian* 16 September 1975, *The Times* 19 September 1975, 6 January 1976
223 *The Guardian* 29 May 1975, 30 May 1975, *The Times* 23 August 1975
224 *Peace News* 9 January 1976, *The Times* 19 December 1975
225 *Peace News* 1 August 1975, *The Times* 7 January 1976
226 *Peace News* 1 August 1975, 29 August 1975, *The Times* 20 September 1975, *Morning Star* 1 October 1975
227 *Time Out* 26 September 1975
228 *Peace News* 5 December 1975
229 S.A. de Smith: *Constitutional and Administrative Law* (London, 1971) pp 205-6
230 David Williams: *Not In The Public Interest* (London, 1965) p 114
231 The prosecution in 1834 was that of the Tolpuddle Martyrs under the *Unlawful Oaths Act 1797,* passed at the same time as the *Incitement to Mutiny Act 1797,* and bearing the same preamble. It is quite clearly related to oaths for seditious purposes, but this was ignored at the trial and the accused were convicted. This was one of the most blatant examples of the revival of obscure statutes for new purposes in the political field.
232 *Hansard (Lords)* 8 November 1934
233 Ralph Miliband: *The State in Capitalist Society* (London, 1969) p 116
234 *ibid* p 123
235 S.P. Huntingdon: *The Soldier and the State* (London, 1964) p 66
236 E.C.S. Wade & Godfrey Phillips: *Constitutional Law* (London, 8th ed. 1970) p 529
237 Harry Street: *Freedom, the Individual and the Law* (London, 3rd ed. 1972) p 210
238 *The Times* 4 July 1975
239 de Smith: *op cit* p 470

THE COBDEN TRUST

The formation of the Cobden Trust in 1963 stemmed directly from the work of the National Council for Civil Liberties (NCCL). The two work in close cooperation and their aims are the same: the protection and extension of civil liberties in Britain.

But while the NCCL is a voluntary organisation which takes up issues and individual cases of injustice, the Cobden Trust is a registered charity undertaking research and education work, creating a deeper understanding of civil liberties.

The future programme of the Trust includes work on duty solicitors schemes (to be published in 1976), prisoners rights, the operation of immigration legislation, and local government and civil liberties.

WITH YOUR HELP . . .

You can help the Trust to do a better job: to do more research and to help more people to know their rights.

While we are able to raise some funds from charitable trusts and foundations, we cannot achieve our purpose without generous public support.

Because the Cobden Trust can recover tax from the Inland Revenue on every £ covenanted, your covenanted contribution will substantially increase the value of your gift.

You are therefore invited to complete the Deed of Covenant and Bankers Order forms on the next page.

Cash donations are also welcomed by the Trust. These can be made out by Bankers Order, or sent directly by cheque to the Secretary.

Deed of Covenant

Name in full I . . . . (Mr/Mrs/Miss)

Address of . . . .

. . . .

. . . .

hereby covenant with the Trustees of the Cobden Trust that for a period of seven years, from the date hereof or during my life, whichever period shall be shorter, I will pay to the Trustees, on the   in each year, such sum as will after deduction of income tax at the current rate leave in the hands of the Cobden Trust the net sum of   such sum being paid from my general fund of taxed income so that I shall receive no personal or private benefit in any of the said years from the said annual payments or of any part thereof. In witness whereof I have hereto set my hand seal this   day of   19

In the presence of witness . . . .

Address . . . .

. . . .

Occupation . . . .

(PLEASE USE CAPITAL LETTERS)

PLEASE SEND THE COMPLETED FORMS TO:

THE SECRETARY, THE COBDEN TRUST, 186 KING'S CROSS ROAD, LONDON WC1X 9DE.

Banker's Order

The Manager . . . .

. . . .

. . . .

(Name and address of bank)

Please pay to credit of the COBDEN TRUST A/C NO. 70355976 as William & Glyn's Bank Ltd, 25 Millbank, London SW1P 4RB, on the day of 19 the sum of and the same sum on the same date each year until 19 and debit my account number accordingly.

(Office use only)

(When making each payment please quote 08107(05))

Name . . . . (Mr/Mrs/Miss)

Address . . . .

. . . .

. . . .

Signature . . . . Date . . . .

Donations

I enclose £ . . . . as a donation to the general work of the Cobden Trust.

Name . . . .

Address . . . .

. . . .

. . . .

Date . . . . 19 . . . .